# More Moral Than God

# More Moral Than God

## Taking Responsibility for Religious Violence

Charlene P. E. Burns

ROWMAN & LITTLEFIELD PUBLISHERS, INC.
*Lanham • Boulder • New York • Toronto • Plymouth, UK*

ROWMAN & LITTLEFIELD PUBLISHERS, INC.

Published in the United States of America
by Rowman & Littlefield Publishers, Inc.
A wholly owned subsidary of The Rowman & Littlefield Publishing Group, Inc.
4501 Forbes Boulevard, Suite 200, Lanham, Maryland 20706
www.rowmanlittlefield.com

Estover Road
Plymouth PL6 7PY
United Kingdom

British Library Cataloguing in Publication Information Available

**Library of Congress Cataloging-in-Publication Data**

Burns, Charlene Embrey, 1953–
   More moral than God : taking responsibility for religious violence / Charlene P.E. Burns.
     p. cm.
   Includes bibliographical references and index.
   ISBN-13: 978-0-7425-5868-7 (cloth : alk. paper)
   ISBN-10: 0-7425-5868-1 (cloth : alk. paper)
   eISBN-13: 978-0-7425-6343-8
   eISBN-10: 0-7425-6343-X
   1. Violence—Religious aspects. 2. Psychology, Religious. I. Title.

   BL65.V55B87 2008
   205'.697—dc22  2008005146

Printed in the United States of America

∞™ The paper used in this publication meets the minimum requirements of American
National Standard for Information Sciences—Permanence of Paper for Printed Library
Materials, ANSI/NISO Z39.48-1992.

For my parents
Charles and Jackie Embrey

# Contents

# Preface

Religion is a pearl of great price . . . a tender plant which gives its finest
flowers only after careful culture . . . liberty is not the only thing whose
price is eternal vigilence.[1]

The causes of violence are myriad and complex, and religiously motivated violence even more so. Violence in the name of religious ideologies is nothing
new, but its potential destructiveness has grown exponentially as technologies
of warfare are made more efficient. Hundreds of books on the subject of religion and violence have been published in recent decades, with a nearly expo-
nential increase in activity since 9/11. The perspectives offered in these works
help us to understand the roles that religious texts, politics, economics, scarcity
of natural resources, history, nationalism, ethnocentrism, social factors, human psychology, and images of the divine play in justification of violence. Although these broad perspectives are important and helpful in providing frameworks for dialogue, they do little to alleviate the personal frustration that many
of us feel in the face of this growing problem. Most of the literature on the
topic falls into one of two categories: attempts to explain the phenomenon or
attempts to identify warning signs before violence breaks out.

The first approach, theorizing which seeks to explain, is important, but it
may be too abstract to speak to persons outside the academy. The second approach is also quite important and certainly helpful to agencies charged with
public safety. This work is distinctive in that, while there is an explanatory
thread running throughout, my ultimate goal is to offer a theoretical framework that moves closer to application than most of the work presently available. I am a theologian with expertise in the psychology of religion and so my
work is in a sense transdisciplinary. Because I inhabit two worlds, so to speak,

I am perhaps in a better position than some theorists to explore the ways religious beliefs and psychological mechanisms interact.

The primary aim of the book is to illuminate the interplay between our images of God, individual egos, and collective selves, and to bring to light the degree to which each of us shares responsibility for transformation of the religious landscape. Because the stance I take in this work is that each of us has a degree of personal responsibility for violence done in the name of religion, it is especially important to clairfy some basic terms.

Even in some of the best writing on the subject today it is common to see "violence" and "terrorism" used as synonyms, and distinctions are rarely made among broad categories of violence. Violence is here defined as "the exercise of physical force so as to inflict injury on, or cause damage to, persons or property; action or conduct characterized by this; treatment or usage tending to cause bodily injury or forcibly interfering with personal freedom" (*Oxford English Dictionary*, 2nd ed.). Terrorism is defined as "violence that is targeted at civilian populations . . . communities, and state institutions with the aim of attracting maximum public attention in order to affect political change or power shifts in favour of the perpetrator's cause."[2] In this framework, not all violence is terrorism, although all terrorism is violence.

Since not all religious violence is terrorism, some important theoretical works, because they concentrate on terrorist acts, will not quite fit the agenda here. Terrorism is a complicated phenomenon affected by many variables. It takes different forms and occurs across political, national, and economic lines. It is done to accomplish many different objectives and is performed by religious and nonreligious people. Central to defining terrorism is the fact that terrorist groups are weaker than their perceived enemies. Also important is their readiness to murder noncombatants in order to achieve their goals.[3] This is important to note because religious violence is often perpetrated not by the weak but by those in power. Examples include the Roman Catholic Church's centuries-long Inquisition and formal warfare declared by religious authorities like the popes in Christian history and Muhammad in Islam. Terrorist psychology may have a lot in common with gang violence, whereas religious violence sanctioned by the powerful may operate through distinctive mechanisms best illuminated by psychoanalysis.

In this work, I take the position that, if we are to get at the root causes of violence in the name of our gods, we must understand the psychology of the individual actor, since this is where violence begins. Obviously, individuals often act most destructively in groups, so social psychology and group dynamics are important, but we must not lose sight of the fact that groups are made up of individuals in this process. Although politics, secularization, globalization, economic conditions, charismatic leadership, disenfranchisement, and many other factors play a role, what matters most is what goes on in the minds of individuals. As we shall see, the subjective experience of injustice or deprivation matters far more than the conditions of objective reality. External factors are necessary but clearly not sufficient conditions for religious violence. Perpetrators of violence do so because of how they *perceive* their situations, which—oddly enough—are often objectively those of middle-class citizens who have the agency and resources necessary to shape their own futures. Many of the popular sociological, political, and economic theories founder on this fact.

I find the archetypal psychoanalytic approach developed by Carl G. Jung to be most promising here. Jung's psychology is robust not only because it is, as we shall see, quite compatible with current trends in cognitive science, psychology, and evolutionary thought. It is enjoying a resurgence of interest for these and other reasons. Archetypal psychology has proven to be heuristically quite powerful. In spite of a tendency among some twentieth-century psychologists to minimize Jung's work, Jungian psychology has had a sustained following among analysts for whom his work enriches other systems and therapeutic approaches. Christian clergy have found Jungian and archetypal psychology to be a rich source of ideas for enhancing the lives of their parishioners. Many intelligent lay people have discovered in archetypal psychology tools for personal transformation. The writings of psychologists like James Hillman and Thomas Moore, among others, have enjoyed a wide readership. Jung's theories speak to a broad cross section of professionals and lay people, perhaps much more so than any other single system of psychoanalytic thought. His work resonates with people's lived experience. Since one goal of this work is to provide conceptual tools for working against the perversion of religious ideologies, use of concepts already proven to speak effectively to nonspecialists is a most reasonable approach. Taken as an interpretive lens, archetypal psychology can help us construct a potentially empowering means for approaching the serious problem of religious violence.

By means of this perspective, I hope to offer an understanding of religion that avoids the simplistic tendency to scapegoat religion in and of itself as the problem. I will show that, while secularization and globalization do play a role, they do so by virtue of the impact on our God-images and in concert with psychological mechanisms related to narcissism. The secularization process often has the effect of destabilizing the God-image within for members of collectivistic cultures, and as we shall see, it is this process that may well provide the necessary and sufficient conditions for religious violence. The relationship between the God-image and the Self is crucial here.

We will need to cover a lot of territory in searching for the root causes of violence in the name of our gods. Some orientation to the broader issues will be necessary to clarify the question. In chapter 1, "Does Religion Cause Violence?" we will engage in a short discussion of the origins of religions. Unless we understand what religion is my claim that it is problematic to assert that religion in and of itself is the cause of violence might be misunderstood. Obviously, since violence is often perpetrated for nonreligious reasons, it is overly simplistic to lay the blame at the feet of "religion." But there is a deeper problem that arises with claims that "religion is violent" or that "religion causes violence." The problem involves the reification of "religion." Reification, the interpretation of phenomena as if they were concrete objects, is to some degree a normal aspect of human psychology, but it can and often does lead us to errors in thinking that cause us to miss deeper aspects of the problem. One serious consequence of reifying religion is that it results in our tendency to make a scapegoat of this intangible construct. The process serves to distance us from any element of personal responsibility and it thereby reduces the likelihood of uncovering lasting solutions to this serious problem. Psychologically speaking, reification can function like a defense mechanism which allows us to avoid responsibility for behaviors and decisions.

Chapter 2 continues orientation of our discussion through a sampling of the history of major acts of religious violence and examination of the role played by sacred scriptures. Misconceptions about the violent nature of some religious traditions continue in spite of the many publications on the subject. The tendency has been to focus on the violent histories of monotheisms, with the spotlight on Islam and Christianity. This has narrowed the attention of theorists and contributed to claims that, if secularization and globalization aren't the source, then scriptures are. The problem of religious violence is rooted in the human psyche, a point which the survey of violence will help to illuminate. I include examples which are less widely known so as to underscore the point that texts are no more acting agents than religions are.

Chapter 3, "Searching for the Roots of 'Religious' Violence," provides a survey of recent nonpsychological explanatory literature. Root causes for religious violence can be found in nearly every aspect of human culture: politics, globalization, the economy, environmental issues, and even biological evolution. We will touch briefly on these concerns, but of special interest here will be claims made by numerous scholars from a variety of disciplines that monotheisms are uniquely and inherently violent. The sampling of religious violence in history will have already demonstrated the error in claiming that monotheisms are uniquely violent, but the claim that "monotheism abhors, reviles, rejects, and ejects whatever it defines as outside its compass" and "forges identity antithetically" in such a way as to lead to violence against outsiders does need to be more directly addressed.[4] Proponents of this view believe the monotheistic image of God is "most potent in terms of social effects" because of its inherent particularism.[5] These claims will be examined in the context of resource scarcity. The chapter concludes with a case study of religious violence in the Philippines which illustrates the interplay of factors and highlights the need to narrow our focus to human psychology.

In the fourth chapter, we examine some of the more important psychological explanations offered for violent religious behaviors. Attention will be given to social psychology but always with the goal of uncovering the dynamics of religious violence at the level of the individual. James W. Jones has noted that while there is a plethora of work published on the psychology of religious violence, very little has been done in terms of psychodynamics.[6] This is unfortunate since psychoanalytic theories provide potent resources for uncovering the factors influencing individual motivation and behavior. For this reason, in chapter 5 we will mine psychoanalysis for useful material and learn how depth psychologies of religion, especially those based in Jungian principles, offer much for developing a deeper understanding.

Chapter 6, "Knowing God, Knowing Ourselves," explores the philosophical and theological premises of archetypal psychology. The chapter offers correction for common misinterpretations of Jungian theories of religion which stem from failure to understand that when Jung wrote of God he was referring only to the image of God, not God *in se*. He believed Immanuel Kant's thesis of the epistemological limitations of knowing (based on a distinction between the phenomenal and noumenal aspects of reality) was the only "honest" way to address metaphysical questions. This is so because, he believed, we can never say anything about God that is free of contamination by our own agendas. Jung's theory of the archetypes, the ego and Self, and the collective unconscious are explained in the context of understanding how individual psychologies influence our images of God. Given that Kant's epistemology has been subjected to criticism for the apparently unbridgeable gap between knowing and being, I offer at this point in the argument a brief excursus on these Kantian concepts to construct a bridge across the divide. Nineteenth-century theologian Friedrich Schleiermacher's critique is of help here. According to Schleiermacher, Kant's gap between mind and matter (which Schleiermacher called the "nullpoint") marks the limits of thought, where a kind of objectless awareness (*Gefühl*) becomes possible. I posit that this state of objectless awareness has been identified by practitioners of many religious traditions, and will explore, in the last chapter, the relationship between it and the process of psychological maturation that Jung called individuation. After a demonstration that Schleiermacher's closing of the gap between the phenomenal and the noumenal provides firmer grounding for Jung's psychology of religion, the chapter proceeds with specifically Jungian themes.

The remainder of this chapter explains Jung's psychology of religion, the relationship between God-images and human psychology, and his claim that our God-images evolve in response to other evolutionary factors. Jung's psychology shows why it is that religious symbols call us to do great good and also great evil. In what has been called Jung's "psychological ethic," humanity must take responsibility for the transformation of our immoral God-images. This can only be accomplished as each of us works toward personal psychological maturity in the context of communal evolution.

In the final chapter, "We Must Become More Moral Than Our Gods," the discussion is summed up. The psychology of idealization and ego inflation added to Carl Jung's claim that "the real history of the world is the progressive incarnation of the deity"[7] leads to the conclusion that our immoral gods can only be transformed by one individual at a time, by each us of becoming more moral than our gods. Since collectivities like religious groups are shaped by the accumulated deep-seated emotional patterns and unacknowledged thoughts of individuals, the problems of groups are accumulations of individual evils. When ego inflation leads to identification of the Self with a reified image of the transcendent, the soil is most fertile for religious violence. We will see, though, that the teachings of many religions provide tools for believers that are designed to lead to states of objectless awareness. These states are described differently among the religions but share the goal of dissolving or overcoming attachment to selfish goals and ego inflation. (This is consonant with, although not identical to, the therapeutic goal of psychological integration and maturation.) As is so often true in human experience, the very systems of thought and belief which are thought to contain the seeds of violence contain also the seeds of peace.

It is my hope that this exploration of the problem of religious violence through the lens of archetypal psychology will enrich the discussion. Perhaps it will inspire a few to see this as a challenge to engage in personal reflection that bears positive fruits for ameliorating the problem of violence. At the very least, I hope it will inspire a new and fruitful line of thinking. This book is the outgrowth of projects funded by the College of Arts and Sciences and the Office of Research and Sponsored Programs, University of Wisconsin–Eau Claire. My interest in writing a book on religious violence grew out of teaching "Religion and Morality," an introductory Religious Studies course I've taught nearly every semester since accepting the teaching position here at UWEC in 2001. In many ways, the inspiration for this book comes from the hundreds of students who have explored with me the relationship between religious teachings on morality and their inversion in practice that so often justifies actions that contradict core beliefs.

First steps toward an actual manuscript began in 2004 with a course-grant from the University Research and Creative Activities program;

additional support came by way of two small Faculty-Student Collaborative Summer Research Grants, one funded in 2004 with Lisa Pinney Johnson and the other in 2007 with Laura J. Jones. The project's completion was ensured by a one-semester sabbatical leave from my teaching responsibilities in the Department of Philosophy and Religious Studies.

The editorial staff of Rowman & Littlefield has provided much appreciated encouragement, expertise, and guidance in shaping the final product. My anonymous reviewers, whose careful readings and astute comments on a first draft of the manuscript have ensured the final product is a much better one, deserve special thanks. Their contributions have been enormously helpful.

More personally, much of my inspiration comes from my son, Tom. The driving force behind all that I do is the hope that my efforts might make some small contribution to bettering the world in which he must live.

## NOTES

1. James B. Pratt, "Religion and the Younger Generation," *Yale Review* 12 (1923): 594–613.

2. Oliver McTernan, *Violence in God's Name: Religion in an Age of Conflict* (Maryknoll, NY: Orbis Books, 2003), xvi.

3. Louise Richardson, "The Roots of Terrorism: An Overview," in *The Roots of Terrorism*, ed. Louise Richardson, Club de Madrid Series on Democracy and Terrorism, vol. 1 (New York: Routledge, 2006), 2.

4. Regina M. Schwartz, *The Curse of Cain: The Violent Legacy of Monotheism* (Chicago: University of Chicago Press, 1997), 16.

5. Rodney Stark, *One True God: Historical Consequences of Monotheism* (Princeton, NJ: Princeton University Press, 2001), 116.

6. James W. Jones, "Why Does Religion Turn Violent? A Psychoanalytic Exploration of Religious Terrorism," *Psychoanalytic Review* 93, no. 2 (April 2006): 167–90.

7. C. G. Jung, *Letters*, 2 vols., trans. R. F. C. Hull, ed. Gerhard Adler and Aniela Jaffé, Bollingen Series 95:1 (Princeton, NJ: Princeton University Press, 1973), 436.

*Chapter One*

# Does Religion Cause Violence?

"All religion is inherently prone to violence. . . . Religion causes violence."[1] "Religion needs to be acknowledged as an actor in its own right."[2] Claims like these have become a trend in recent scholarship on religion, including everything from religious violence to the evolutionary origins of religions. The awareness that violence and religious ideologies are often connected is not new, but our sense of urgency in finding ways to break that bond has become intense as the capacity for widespread devastation becomes more accessible to all sorts of people. In 2006, for example, a Michigan teenager succeeded in building "the business end of a hydrogen bomb" from parts he bought on eBay and at the local hardware store.[3] If an American teenager can accomplish this, imagine what highly motivated and educated adults who believe it is their religious duty to eliminate others can do. It is the stuff of nightmares.

By the time we reach the end of these first chapters you may well be inclined to agree with those who claim religion itself is a major source of violence. It is my hope, however, that by the final chapters you will have developed an understanding of the complexity of this issue. Since one aspect of my thesis here is that each of us can and must share some degree of responsibility for transformation of the religious landscape,we must begin with a caution regarding language. Claims that religion is "an actor in its own right" or that it "causes violence" are subtly misleading and reveal that we have made a mistake in logical thinking. This mistake is called the "fallacy of misplaced concreteness"[4] whereby we have treated an abstract concept as though it were a concrete entity having agency in its own right. Sometimes called reification, this manner of speaking enables us to make a scapegoat of an abstraction. Scapegoating a concept like religion allows us to distance ourselves from the issues and reduces or eliminates our sense of personal responsibility. This

1

process is very important and we need to understand how it works, so before surveying the history of religious violence, we need to examine this tendency to reify intangibles after grounding ourselves with a quick study of how cultures and social realities like religions develop.

## CULTURAL DEVELOPMENT
## AND THE ORIGIN OF RELIGIONS

In order to understand the relation between religion and violence it helps to understand something about the way religions develop within human cultures, and how we experience cultures. Human existence is paradoxical in that society is a product of human activity over the course of time, and yet we experience it as "given," as always-already-there. We are born, in other words, into preconstructed social worlds that appear to have objective reality. Cultures and societies confront us as realities that exist outside our own consciousness: culture is simply "there," and the material and nonmaterial objectives of it are shared among people.[5] The human being is "an open system continuously engaged in mutual development with the outside."[6] A person is able to step outside of her subjective world into the realm of shared creation, from which cultures and religions come.

Nearly all human mental abilities are found to some degree in other species, but the capacity for formation of elaborate cultures and complex relationships seems to be uniquely ours. Humans are actually very similar to other primates in terms of our biological relation to cognition. The major difference seems to be that we identify with fellow humans more deeply than other primates appear to identify to their fellows. One chimp will see the outcome of another chimp's behavior and try to replicate it, as do human children. Chimps, however, apparently cannot understand the connection between the other primate's behavior and the outcome, whereas humans as young as two years old focus more on the strategy used by others. We understand the other as an intentional agent having a mental life like our own, and we try to understand things from the other's standpoint, while the chimp sees the outcome and strives to get there from within his own mental world.[7] This supports claims that human beings are much more dependent upon others: "The human brain is the only brain in the biosphere whose potential cannot be realized on its own."[8] We are essentially cultural beings.

Evolutionary biology, anthropology, and psychology tell us that the dramatic evolution of cognitive skills in the human cannot have occurred without the simultaneous development of culture. Our extremely complex brains have developed in ways that assume the existence of an external means for pooling cognitive resources. By means of symbol systems like language, human minds can learn "not just *from* the other [as other species do] but *through* the other."[9] Cultures are ecologies that function as storehouses that make it possible for humans to share learning, language, religious beliefs, and customs across generations. The "symbolic technologies" of our cultures "liberate consciousness from the limitations of the brain's biological memory systems" and enable us to break the bonds of biology.[10] Religions, as products of this process, are created through the interaction of human symbolic technologies and our experiences of subjectivity and objectivity.

All cultures evolve powerful underlying systems through which groups of people organize social experience, knowledge, and activity within the social world. These "folk psychologies" are inherently tied to morality in that they communicate to us, not just how things are, but also how they ought to be. The folk psychology is used to communicate the canons of a culture from one generation to the next. This is accomplished primarily through narrative. In the telling of stories to our children, we ensure that the next generation understands how and why things are as they are. The basic principles of a folk psychology narrative assume that (1) people have beliefs and desires that relate us to the past, present, and future; (2) these beliefs come together to produce commitments and dispositions; (3) there is an external world that modifies our expression of beliefs and desires; (4) we have knowledge of the world that shapes our beliefs and desires; and (5) human beings are complex creatures capable of exercising agency.[11]

Human societies are constructed as we externalize our beliefs and desires through narrative, distance ourselves from these aspects of experience, and then internalize the "objective" structures that result from this social process. Distancing ourselves from these externalized aspects makes it possible for us to establish relationships with our world and others. The socially created world imposes upon us expectations and roles which we internalize so as to make them our own. Our identities are shaped by this socialization process. This is not a passive process—we actively appropriate the social world and thus shape our identities. We coproduce the social world and ourselves in a never-ending process of socialization. "Social structure is produced by [humans] and in turn produces [us]."[12] Ironically, even though we are active participants in the process, we are most often not conscious of it.

A culture's folk psychology provides the template for the process by which each of us develops our own particular worldviews. Religious traditions have historically made up major powerful portions of the most enduring aspects of cultural folk psychologies and so are foundational aspects of the basic worldview for many. Because religious teachings are so foundational to our worldviews and so influential in human behavior, many people claim that religion is itself a central cause of violence. Just what are religions, though? Why are the ideas communicated through them so compelling and influential in human history?

## DEFINING "RELIGION"

Religion is notoriously difficult to define. It is one of those terms that offer special challenges: we are certain we know what religion is until someone asks for a clear definition. A clear, succinct definition is one that tells what, not why, religion is, without implying judgment, and is broad enough to encompass all religions but not so broad as to be meaningless. How one defines it depends to a great extent on one's purpose in doing so. Since our concern in this book is to examine the problem of violence done in the name of religious traditions, a functional definition will prove most useful. We want to understand how religious people come to justify violent actions in the service of their beliefs, so understanding something of how religions function generally will be an important step toward the goal.

One reason we find religion so difficult to define may arise from the fact that in many cultures there is no term that designates a realm of the spiritual that can be identified apart from other aspects of life. The idea that religion is distinct and separable from the rest of life seems to be a particularly Western view, perhaps an outcome of the Protestant Reformation, the rise of science in seventeenth- and eighteenth-century Europe, and the "separation of church and state" principle held so dear in the United States. The name "Jew," for example, was coined by the ancient Romans in the first century BCE as a way of speaking about a group of people who lived in the coastal regions at the eastern end of the Mediterranean Sea. "Judaism," then, originally indicated the way of life practiced by those who lived in Judea, and not their religion, per se. Likewise, for most of the world's citizens even today, the idea that their beliefs about that which is sacred and spiritual should be held apart from other aspects of life is incomprehensible. To paraphrase Gandhi, anyone who imagines that religion and other aspects of life, especially politics, can and ought to be separated clearly understands neither. This is so because religious systems are about making sense of existence. Our religious beliefs are among the basic building blocks of our worldviews and as such necessarily inform all aspects of life.

Our worldviews function for us very much like lenses or windows through which all experience is filtered. The materials from which our worldviews are constructed shape what we see and how we interpret it. Worldviews are made up of family, social, and cultural teachings absorbed from the time we are born. This process happens for the most part unconsciously, and many people never stop to consider just what materials have come to make up the window through which they view the world. Think of worldviews as windows made of many different kinds of glass. Not all glass allows us to see the world outside clearly. Very old glass, for example, usually has bubbles and distortions in it that make the world outside appear off-kilter. Tinted glass may allow a relatively good view but can make it hard to tell whether it's sunny or cloudy outside. Stained glass makes for a magnificent aesthetic experience but allows us to see little or nothing of what is on the other side. The kind of materials out of which our worldviews are constructed determines to a great degree how we view the world and what we can even see. Religious beliefs are among the most influential of worldview construction resources.

The religious systems that have evolved in human history vary widely in their claims about things like the origins of the universe and the purpose of human existence. It is accurate, though, to say that all systems labeled "religious" share at least two claims. First, religious systems claim that this material existence is not all there is—there exists another dimension of reality that in some sense is more "real" or perfect than the present life. This "something more" is often called the spiritual dimension. Second, religious systems contain moral codes of conduct, or ethical teachings that instruct believers in the proper way to live this life so as to realize the spiritual dimension of the faith once this bodily existence is terminated.

All of this is to say that religious systems, regardless of how they may differ, help us to find meaning in existence and provide guidance for how we ought to live. A meaning system is made up of the beliefs that an individual constructs about herself, others, and the world; a meaning system provides order to life. Religions are unique among meaning-making systems in that they are comprehensive (explain everything from creation to the end of existence), centered on the spiritual dimension, and offer answers to the deepest questions of existence (e.g., Why is there something rather than nothing? What happens after I die?).

Religion is especially powerful in times of crisis. This is so because for most practitioners' religious beliefs provide ways for making sense of and finding value in trauma or experiences of injustice. It is an odd truth that when faced with circumstances that contradict our constructed meaning systems, we are more likely to change our perceptions of the events than to change our religious beliefs. Religious systems are remarkably stable in the face of contradictory information.[13] Religious teachings are central to believers' worldviews and provide the scaffolding upon which meaning is constructed. It is understandable, then, that these structures so often seem to have a life independent of the human individuals and groups which give rise to them, but claims that religions "cause violence" are deceptive products of mistaken logic. This fallacy of reification, wherein the abstract concept "religion" is treated as though it has agency in its own right, is an important issue that must be addressed in our efforts to understand violence done in the name of sacred realties.

## REIFICATION, SOCIAL CONSTRUCTION, AND PERSONAL RESPONSIBILITY

Reification, the interpretation of phenomena as if they were concrete objects, is to some degree a normal aspect of human psychology. If not critically examined, however, this tendency can lead us to errors in thinking that cause us to miss deeper characteristics of problems at hand. Phrases which imply that religion is itself an acting agent, apart from human beings who believe in religious ideas, are the end result of processes through which we construct societies and cultures.

As noted previously, we remain unconscious of the process for the most part, and so we "forget" that we are ourselves the producers of our social and cultural worlds. In the forgetting, aspects of our constructed social realities take on the character of "otherness." This sense of otherness results in our experience of these constructed realities as having an ontological status and a power of their own. Intangible concepts, in other words, become "things" about which we talk as though they are independent actors having real agency outside our control.[14] This is the process of reification. Peter Gabel explains:

> We participate in an unconscious conspiracy with others whereby everyone knows of the fallacy, and yet denies the fallacy exists . . . reification is not simply a form of distortion but also a form of unconscious coercion which, on the one hand, separates the communicated or socially apparent reality from the reality of experience, and, on the other hand, denies this separation is taking place.[15]

Through reification, social roles (fatherhood, the presidency), institutions (the government, the family), and ideologies (religion, democracy, socialism) are first defined by us but over time come to embody abstractions that define us. Reification of intangible aspects of human existence like these limits our choices and serves to prescribe our actions. Social injustices have often been the end result of this process.

Although reification is a natural, ubiquitous, and unconscious process, it is not a necessity. In fact, de-reification has happened often in human history. De-reification becomes possible under certain circumstances: (1) when social structures disintegrate, due to natural disasters or devastating warfare; (2) when cultures "clash" through migration or, as is happening today, through globalization; and (3) when marginalized individuals or groups work to confront the status quo.[16]

Much of the current conversation about religious violence revolves around a reified understanding of religion and of writings considered sacred, usually referred to as scriptures. As we have now seen, once intangibles like "religion" become reified, our experience is that the concepts have taken on "lives of their own." In the minds of many, "religion" has become an independent actor that makes choices and governs our lives; we seem to be helpless in the face of it. This reification of religion is to some degree similar to the way the term "Negro" has functioned in American society. This is one example that helps clarify the power and danger of reification. Before the 1950s and 1960s in the United States, the socially accepted understanding of "Negro" included the belief that people who belonged to this group were not intelligent or responsible enough to exercise the right to vote, regardless of age, education, or economic status. The participants in the Civil Rights Movement knew that their efforts had to offer a deliberate and conscious challenge to this conception in order to effect real change. It was because the person and work of a man like Martin Luther King Jr. challenged this reified notion that many people came to see the injustice of American voting laws and practices clearly. Hopefully, the exposition on individual psychology and religious experience offered in the final chapters of this book will allow a glimpse at the core of healthy spirituality that might explain the power of men like King to undermine a centuries-old reified concept.

I do not intend to convey the idea that one ought never to reify any concept or that we must stamp it out wherever we find it. One very important positive function of the process is that it serves to enhance communication. What I am advocating here is that we strive to become conscious of it and learn to apply the principle of parsimony to its use. Parsimonious use would require that we not speak concretely of immaterial or nonobservable entities unless doing so contributes greatly to our comprehension of phenomena that would otherwise be inexplicable.[17] There are times when reification is helpful; in our case this is particularly true when speaking of psychological mechanisms. In a sense, all theoretical psychological structures are reified postulates. One example is the Jungian concept of archetypes, which are universal motifs that account for common themes in human myths, dreams, and religions. The concept will be very important to the constructive portion of my thesis, and if it weren't for the ability to reify this concept to a degree, it would be impossible to explain what I mean. However, I do not (and neither did Jung) intend to imply that archetypes are actual physical entities literally located in the human brain.

When it comes to "religion" and to scriptures though, in this context, the problems of reification far outweigh the benefits. If "religion" itself is the cause of violence, what possible recourse do we have? This impersonal intangible entity is wreaking havoc in our world, and we are impotent in the face of it, since we find no one who can be held accountable. Reified religion leads us to make unrealistic claims and offer impracticable solutions to the problem of violence like, "Religion has killed more people than any other idea so it should be eliminated."

## "THE SCRIPTURES MADE ME DO IT"

Although not all of them go so far as to agree that religious violence is "first and foremost a problem of 'sacred texts' and not a problem of misinterpretation,"[18] a number of scholars have theorized in recent years that a major causative factor is to be found in these writings. The problematic nature of violence in the sacred records has long been recognized; as early as the first century, Jewish scholars worked to explain the violence of the Bible. In the Middle Ages, the Christian theologian Thomas Aquinas wrote that the warfare recorded in the scriptures ought to be interpreted "'mystically,'" not literally.[19] Phyllis Trible was among the first scholars in recent times to call attention to the "texts of terror" in the Hebrew Bible. Her specific agenda was to read the tales of violence against women through a feminist lens so as to subvert it, or as she put it, "to recover a neglected history, to remember a past that in the present embodies, and to pray that these terrors shall not come to pass again."[20]

In the decades following the publication of Trible's book, scholars and theologians sympathetic to Judaism and Christianity worked hard to find ways to reinterpret scriptural violence. Today we find all sorts of explanations or justifications in the literature, offering a wide range of claims. Some say that the violence is merely a rhetorical device never meant to motivate or justify violence against others. Others claim that, given that the majority of violence found in the Hebrew Bible is committed at the direction of or in service to God, this means that *God* is the warrior and so "we can be peacemakers."[21] In a similar vein, it has been said that New Testament violence "shows that God's 'violence' is a precondition of human nonviolence."[22]

Anthropologist Hector Avalos argues that all religion is prone to violence. Since most violence is due to conflict over real or imagined scarce resources, religions that create new scarce resources are most likely to be a source of bloodshed.[23] A resource is considered scarce if it is not readily available or if gaining access to and maintaining the resource requires the expenditure of considerable amounts of physical or social labor and capital. Religious vio-

lence is especially heinous for Avalos because, he says, "religious conflict relies solely on resources whose scarcity is wholly manufactured by, or reliant
on, unverifiable premises." He does not claim that religious ideas are the
source of all violence, but he does claim that "when religion causes violence,
it usually does so because it has created a scarce resource."[24] (Note how thoroughly Avalos has reified religion.)

For Avalos all religious systems, not just the monotheisms, generate
scarcity of resources like scripture, salvation, and sacred space.[25] Avalos also
claims that secular philosophies have not served as motivation for violence as
clearly as religious ideologies have, but this is not defensible in the face of
modern history.[26] The American and French Revolutions, the Communist
Revolutions of Russia and China, World Wars I and II, the Vietnam War, Pol
Pot's regime in Cambodia, the U.S. invasions of Iraq—these are just a few examples of violence in the name of secular ideologies. Avalos does, however,
serve us well by reminding us that religious ideas lead to perceived scarcity
of resources in a variety of ways, even if his claim that the "unverifiability"
of God's thoughts about peace and warfare is "the most scarce resource of all,
and a prime generator of violence" is a bit confusing.[27]

The assertion that religious violence is "first and foremost" a problem that
arises from the fact that scriptures contain tales of brutality implies that the
texts themselves exert direct control over human behavior. Sacred texts have
been used by many religious people to justify violence, but it is no more helpful to reify scriptures than it is to imbue "religion" with agency and power independent of the humans who produce the texts and participate in religious
practices. Violence and its justification are found in many of the world's
scriptures, but as we shall see, so are very clear admonitions to make peace
and practice compassion.

A particularly compelling counterargument for a direct and causative correlation between the violence in Hebrew scriptures and the history of violence
in the tradition has been set out by Rabbi Jeremy Milgrom, founder of Clergy
for Peace and consultant to Rabbis for Human Rights. He points out that these
claims are overly simplistic and says they arise from lack of knowledge about
synagogue life and practice. Daily worship in Judaism relies first on the
prayer book, not the Bible. The texts which determine "religious jurispru-
dence" are found in the Talmud (rabbinic commentary on and interpretation
of the scriptures). Rabbi Milgrom argues that, although the Bible certainly is
central to establishment of Jewish ways of life, its impact is perhaps much
more indirect than those who blame the text for human violence realize. In
synagogue worship, there is an annual cycle of reading three to five chapters
of the Torah (first five books of the Bible) each Sabbath. The rest of the Bible
is used less frequently. Psalms and some chapters from the writings of the

prophets are used in weekly worship and daily prayer, but it is not common for Jewish people to read scripture on their own, independently of formal study. This is very different from the way Christians use their scriptures.[28]

As has often been said, the same texts that are filled with violence also teach emphatically that the Lord abhors violence and that warfare is not the solution to human problems. Psalms 20 and 33, for example, tell us that those who "boast of chariots . . . will collapse and fall," that "a king is not saved by his great army; a warrior is not delivered by his great strength." Psalm 46 says that the Lord "makes wars cease . . . breaks the bow, and shatters the spear." And of course, the description in Isaiah of the kingdom of God to be inaugurated by the coming of the messiah is that of a peaceful world: The nations "shall beat their swords into plowshares and their spears into pruning hooks; nation shall not lift up sword against nation, neither shall they learn war any more" (Isaiah 2:4). These passages quoted here provide a few examples of admonitions to nonviolence found in the very texts which are often blamed for violence. Claims for a direct correlation between scriptural violence and acts in the present day are too reductionist and simplistic, an issue explored more fully at the end of this chapter. Whatever one may believe about inspiration for the texts, the scriptures were written by human beings and record violent acts committed by humans.

In actuality, it is very hard to support claims for a direct correlation between violence in scriptures and acts of violence in history. We will see that the history of Buddhism is replete with violence even though its vast corpus of scripture contains far more instruction about peace, loving-kindness, and avoidance of violence than support for war and killing. The first of Buddhism's Five Precepts for lay people is ahimsa, noninjury. In several of the texts, the Buddha is quoted as saying directly that one must never do harm to other living beings, not even with our angry thoughts or harsh words. The Brahmajala Sutta (date of origin is unclear) states that no follower of the Buddha may participate in any form of violence, not even indirectly. In spite of myriad texts that insist on nonviolence, Buddhists have managed to find ways to justify conducting war in the service of transcendent goals. This is so because people make choices which lead to violence. Those choices may begin with interpretation of scripture or with the desire to possess resources that are in the hands of others. Whatever the justification for it, human beings, not scriptural texts and not "religion," are the acting agents when violence occurs.

Hector Avalos has said, for example, that "the best way to deal with religious violence is to undermine religion itself." Religion is such a powerful entity for Avalos that he goes so far as to insist that undermining it should be the agenda of academic religious studies![29] While it is certainly true that the tendency among textual scholars has in the past been to gloss over the violence in many of the world's scriptures, it is clearly not appropriate for the academician to undertake a program of destruction of our students' beliefs. Avalos is correct in criticizing the tendency to ignore the dark side of religious texts and traditions, but academics are charged with the responsibility of educating, not indoctrinating, our students. Besides, even if one were to agree that human societies might be better off without religion, how would one go about eliminating it? So if we agree with Avalos, we are left feeling helpless and, even more dangerously, free of personal responsibility when reified views of religion prevail.

We live today in a time that is ripe for de-reifying this concept. Some claim that social structures around the world seem to be weakening. Through globalization radically different cultures are coming face-to-face. This contact is breaking down the assurance that "our way is the only way." And, at least in the United States, voices from the fringes are becoming louder in their objections to the growing gap between rich and poor, to American foreign policies which lead to military invasion and occupation of other nations, and other issues related to social injustices committed in the name of national security. In what follows I hope to further the de-reification that is already under way.

Our challenge throughout the rest of this study will be to remain vigilant so that we may learn to resist the pull of reification when appropriate. If we succumb to its pull, we abdicate responsibility. If we are to uncover ways by which each of us might make a difference, we must do our best to remember that "religion *as* religion cannot in and of itself be an independent source of violence."[30]

## NOTES

1. Hector Avalos, *Fighting Words: The Origins of Religious Violence* (New York: Prometheus Books, 2005), 18, 21.

2. Oliver McTernan, *Violence in God's Name: Religion in an Age of Conflict* (Maryknoll, NY: Orbis Press, 2003), xv.

3. Stephen Ornes, "Radioactive Boy Scout: Teenager Achieves Nuclear Fusion at Home," *Discover Magazine*, http://discovermagazine.com/2007/mar/radioactive-boy-scout.3.06.2007 (accessed March 30, 2007).

4. Alfred North Whitehead, *Science and the Modern World* (New York: Macmillan, 1925), 75–77.

5. Peter L. Berger, *The Sacred Canopy: Elements of a Sociological Theory of Religion* (Garden City, NY: Doubleday, 1967), 10.

6. Gilbert J. Rose, "The Creativity of Everyday Life," in *Between Fantasy and Reality: Transitional Objects and Phenomena*, ed. Simon Grolnick and Leonard Barkin (New York: Jason Aronson, 1978), 358.

7. Michael Tomasello, *The Cultural Origins of Human Cognition* (Cambridge, MA: Harvard University Press, 1999), 14–30.

8. Merlin Donald, *A Mind So Rare: The Evolution of Human Consciousness* (New York: W. W. Norton, 2001), 324.

9. Tomasello, *Cultural Origins*, 6.

10. Donald, *A Mind So Rare*, 305–6.

11. Jerome Bruner, *Acts of Meaning* (Cambridge, MA: Harvard University Press, 1990), 35–42.

12. Peter Berger and Stanley Pullberg, "Reification and the Sociological Critique of Consciousness," *History and Theory* 4, no. 2 (1965): 202.

13. Crystal Park, "Religion and Meaning," in *Handbook of the Psychology of Religion and Spirituality*, ed. Raymond F. Paloutzian and Crystal Park (New York: Guilford Press, 2005), 295–314.

14. Peter L. Berger and Thomas Luckmann, *The Social Construction of Reality: A Treatise in the Sociology of Knowledge* (New York: Anchor Books, 1967), 88.

15. Peter Gabel, "Reification in Legal Reasoning," in *Research in Law and Sociology*, ed. S. Spencer, vol. 3 (Greenwich, CT: JAI Press, 1980); quoted in Christopher May, "The Denial of History: Reification, Intellectual Property Rights, and the Lessons of the Past," *Class and Capital* 88 (March 2006): 43.

16. Berger and Pullberg, "Reification and the Sociological Critique," 210–11.

17. Eric Gillett, "The Confusion over Personification and Reification," *Psychoanalysis and Contemporary Thought* 16, no. 1 (1993): 3–42.

18. Jack Nelson-Pallmeyer, *Is Religion Killing Us? Violence in the Bible and the Quran* (New York: Trinity Press International, 2003), xiv.

19. Hector Avalos, *Fighting Words: The Origins of Religious Violence* (New York: Prometheus, 2005), 159–60.

20. Phyllis Trible, *Texts of Terror: Literary-Feminist Readings of Biblical Narrative* (Philadelphia: Fortress Press, 1984), 3.

21. Paul Keim, "Is God Non-Violent?" *Conrad Grabel Review* 21, no. 1 (Winter 2003): 27; quoted in Avalos, *Fighting Words*, 164.

22. Miroslav Volf, "Divine Violence?" Letter to the editor, *Christian Century*, October 13, 1999, 972.

23. Hector Avalos, "Rethinking Religious Violence," in *The Just War and Jihad: Violence in Judaism, Christianity, and Islam*, ed. R. Joseph Hoffmann (Amherst, NY: Prometheus, 2006), 100.

24. Avalos, *Fighting Words*, 18–22.

25. Avalos, *Fighting Words*, 83.

26. Avalos, *Fighting Words*, 301.

27. Avalos, *Fighting Words*, 170.

28. Jeremy Milgrom, "'Let Your Love for Me Vanquish Your Hatred for Him': Nonviolence and Modern Judaism," in *Subverting Hatred: The Challenge of Nonviolence in Religious Traditions*, ed. Daniel L. Smith-Christopher (Maryknoll, NY: Orbis Books, 1998), 116–17.

29. Avalos, "Rethinking Religious Violence," 116.

30. T. K. Oommen, "Religion as Source of Violence: A Sociological Perspective," *Ecumenical Review* 53, no. 2 (2001): 168–78.

## Chapter Two

# A Brief History of Religious Violence

Most Westerners are very familiar with some of the more violent episodes in Christian and Islamic history. It is not uncommon for people to assume that these two traditions are responsible for most if not all religious violence, or at least that they are among a very few religious traditions within which violence has regularly occurred. We will see that this is unfortunately not correct; violence in the name of transcendent goals has been quite widespread across the religions and the centuries. The following provides only a sampling of some of the more violent episodes, ancient and modern, in the histories of several major religious systems of thought. The reader who would like a more in-depth study of the violent historical record of these traditions will find ample resources listed in the bibliography.

### HINDUISM

The Hindu traditions are among the world's most ancient religious systems. Origins of the Hindu ways are obscure, but scholars agree that some form of Hinduism has existed in the Indian subcontinent at least since the founding of the Harappa culture in northwestern India around 2000 BCE. The supreme goal of Hindu practice, release from the cycle of rebirth through reincarnation (moksha), is achieved when one's soul (jiva) ceases to be reborn and becomes one with the Absolute Reality (the Brahman). A Hindu achieves moksha by accumulating sufficient positive karma primarily through observing one's dharma. Living according to one's own religious duty is vital: "Your own duty done imperfectly is better than another man's done well," says the god Krishna in the third chapter of the *Bhagavad Gita*, which is the most widely known of the Hindu scriptures.[1]

The *Bhagavad Gita* is most often cited as the source of Hindu attitudes toward violence. The text tells the story of a warrior, Arjuna, who is troubled by the fact that his family is preparing for battle against their cousins. Arjuna discusses his reluctance to fight with his chariot driver who, unbeknownst to Arjuna, is Krishna, an avatar (incarnation) of the god Vishnu. Arjuna says it is wrong to kill one's own family for any reason (BG 1.26–47), but Krishna argues that he must go to war. The god offers two compelling justifications for warfare even against one's own relations:

> Arjuna, when a man knows the self to be indestructible, enduring, unborn, unchanging, how does he kill or cause anyone to kill? As a man discards worn-out clothes to put on new and different ones, so the embodied self discards its worn-out bodies to take on new ones. . . . It cannot be cut or burned; it cannot be wet or withered; it is enduring, all-pervasive, fixed, immovable, and timeless (BG 2.21–24). . . . Look to your own duty; do not tremble before it; nothing is better for a warrior than a battle of sacred duty . . . if you fail to wage this war of sacred duty, you will abandon your own duty . . . only to gain evil (BG 2.31–33).

Since the essence of the self does not die and it is his dharma to fight, not only must Arjuna engage in war against his own family, but also he may kill with impunity.

Although Hindu sacred texts seem fairly unambiguous on the use of violence when doing so fits with one's dharma, there is a significant strand of teachings on the importance of *ahimsa*, living with the intent to do no harm to any being. In fact, the very text which teaches the Hindu that duty may mean conducting warfare against one's relatives also says that knowledge of the true meaning of reality requires nonviolence, among other virtues (BG 13.7; 16.2; 17.14). There are many sacred texts that extol the virtue of noninjury. How does the Hindu reconcile these texts with the teachings on violence? According to traditional interpretation, the presence of teachings for and against violence in the same scripture is only an apparent contradiction. The injunction to practice noninjury and at the same time be willing to kill for the sake of one's duty is taken to mean that in one's personal conduct ahimsa is the ideal, but one must be prepared to use violence when necessary to sustain the social order. Dharma provides social stability, and whatever maintains balance must be seen as one's duty.

The ideal Hindu society is described in the most ancient sacred writings as a class hierarchy of priests (Brahmin), warrior kings (Kshatriya), craftsmen and farmers (Vaishya), and servants (Shudra), with an outcaste classification whose function it is to do the so-called unclean jobs necessary in any human society. Although there is tremendous variation among Hindu sects, they all tend to accept that one's religious duty (dharma) is determined by the requirements of caste, stage of life, and gender.

The caste structure gives shape to politics in the history of India. The Kshatriya have historically had the responsibility for all governing functions. According to the scriptures, the king's role was to ensure social order through policing and administering justice, as well as protecting from external threats through the use of military means. The king's power was always constrained by the higher caste Brahmin priests who served to guide the king in maintaining his connection to the principle of dharma. The ideal king was guided in all things by the Brahmin. This partnership between the highest religious and civil authorities served to legitimate the state and provide protection for the religious authority.[2] And so, violence is acceptable when committed in order "to protect men of virtue, and destroy men who do evil" (BG 4.8). According to the scriptures, "Whatever a king does is right, that is a settled rule; because the protection of the world is entrusted to him . . . a ruler though worthless must be constantly worshiped by his subjects."[3] On the basis of this and other texts, Hinduism has at times been interpreted to legitimate absolute and even dictatorial rulers.

In the twentieth century India saw the outworking of two divergent interpretations of the scriptural record, one leading to a call for nonviolence and the other to the purification of India through whatever means necessary. Mahatma Gandhi (1869–1948) came to believe that the *Bhagavad Gita* was best read as an allegory of the struggle against evil in the human heart, not as a text that legitimates violence. In his own translation and commentary on the text, Gandhi said, "I do not agree that the *Gita* advocates and teaches violence in any part. . . . The fact is that a literal interpretation of the *Gita* lands one in a sea of contradictions . . . it is pre-eminently a description of the duel that goes on in our own hearts."[4] Gandhi taught that *satyagraha*, holding onto truth (which he sometimes called soul-force or love-force), and *ahimsa* are the means by which we overcome injustice. Grounded in his nonliteral reading of Hindu (and Christian) scripture, Gandhi developed a program of nonviolent resistance to political oppression which succeeded in bringing independence to India after centuries of foreign domination by Muslim and British rulers. Ironically, he was assassinated on January 30, 1948, by a man who believed the *Gita* requires violence in order to preserve India as a Hindu nation.

During the past thirty years there has been a dramatic increase in Hindu nationalist movements advocating the return to ancient ways. These ways include strict adherence to the caste system and removal of non-Hindus from positions of power. These Hindutva movements teach that Hinduism is the "mother of all religions." As such, it has nothing to learn from and much to teach to other religions. Hindutva advocates argue that nonviolence is effeminate and contrary to the true nature of Hinduism. Some claim that these teachings are to blame for the centuries-long subjugation of India by foreign powers.⁵ Anti-Christian and anti-Muslim violence is becoming more common throughout India and is justified by appeal to a literal reading of scriptures like the texts quoted above from the *Bhagavad Gita*.

## JUDAISM

The origins of Judaism, like Hinduism, are somewhat obscure. It probably grew out of a henotheistic tradition around 1800–1700 BCE. In a henotheism, one accepts the existence of other gods, while believing in the primacy of one Supreme Being. Our only source of information for the earliest stages of the faith is the Hebrew Bible, the historical accuracy of which is a subject of intense debate. The scriptures portray the development of monotheistic Judaism as a gradual achievement attained through the efforts of the prophets to teach the people the error of their ways in worshipping pagan gods and goddesses. Much has been written in recent times on the subject of violence in the Hebrew Bible. The book of Exodus tells us that "the Lord is a man of war," "majestic" and "terrible in glorious deeds" of conquest (New Revised Standard Version, Exodus 15:3, 11). The scriptures are filled with stories of battle and destruction of human life done in the name of the Lord. Because there was no compartmentalization of life into secular and sacred, the ancient Israelites understood every aspect of existence as the outworking of the Lord's will, so it makes sense that the record of ancient violence portrays these acts as divinely guided.

According to the stories in the scriptures, the threat of violence enters into the picture at the very beginning of creation by an act of God. When Adam and Eve, the first humans, are expelled from the Garden of Eden for having disobeyed divine commands, the gates to the Garden are blocked by the cherubim holding "a flaming sword which turned every way" (Genesis 3:24). The first human act of violence, murder of his brother, is committed by Adam and Eve's son Cain, and it is all downhill from there. God becomes displeased with what turns out to be a human propensity for violence and attempts to eradicate the problem by bringing about a flood which destroys all life except for a chosen few. Unfortunately, this does not work, and God is resigned to the fact that "the imagination of man's heart is evil from his youth" (Genesis 8:21). The first divine-human covenant, made with Noah, is that God will never again destroy all life by flooding the earth. The next covenant is made with Abram/Abraham who becomes the first biblical war hero. The Abrahamic covenant consists of a divine promise to "make of [Abraham] a great nation" (Genesis 12:1–2). From this point on, the biblical record is filled with battles aimed at conquest of the Promised Land, internecine struggles for control, and wars to fend off invading forces. Once the Israelites become established in the region known today as Israel, the struggle to hold the territory intensifies.

Since the historical accuracy of the information in the scriptures is contested by some biblical scholars today, only those major ancient wars documented in extra-biblical sources will be mentioned here. The history of the Middle East is rife with warfare, much of which has had religious undertones. The land was strategically quite valuable, located on the Mediterranean coast and "on the way" to northern Africa, a fertile region rich in natural resources. Prior to the expulsion of the Jews from the region in 135 CE by the Romans and since the 1948 United Nations declaration of Israel as an independent nation, conflict in the region has been fueled by the claim to territory as part of the divine covenant.

In the ninth to eighth centuries BCE several major invasions by the Assyrians occurred which may have involved the deportation of significant numbers of people in 722–721 BCE. The end result was that the formerly independent nation of Israel was reduced to a vassal state of Assyria,[6] while Judah, the southern kingdom, survived independently for a time. In 586 BCE the Babylonians invaded and took many into exile in Babylonia. After about fifty years another great military power, the Persians, defeated Babylonia and allowed the captive Jews to return to their homelands. Invasions continued off and on over the centuries until the region was conquered by the armies of Alexander the Great in the fourth century BCE.

A major rebellion by the Jews against their conquerors occurred in 167 BCE and led to a century of self rule. Unfortunately, once the Jewish people were freed of foreign occupation, internecine violence broke out in response to disagreements over the proper means of governance of the nation of Israel. Some believed the Jewish people should be ruled by a king, in keeping with neighboring territories; some believed the proper authority to be the high priest. Power passed back and forth between kings and priests over the decades between the end of the revolt led by Judas Maccabeus in 167 BCE and 63 BCE, when control of the territory was taken by the Romans.

The period of Roman governance was a turbulent time. Jewish hopes for divine intervention to end foreign oppression grew dramatically, with some claiming the Messiah would come as a great general to lead a military revolution, and others claiming that the Messiah would come as a priestly figure. Small-scale violent revolts and protests were frequent throughout the decades from 63 BCE to 66 CE. There were also small-scale efforts at nonviolent resistance during this period. Writing in the late first century, the historian Josephus (c. 38–100 CE) reported unarmed Jewish demonstrations against Pontius Pilate (Roman governor from 26 to 36 CE) on two occasions. The first involved Pontius Pilate's ordering images of the emperor on military standards to be placed in Jerusalem. In Josephus's words,

Multitudes of excited Jews rushed to Caesarea to petition him for the removal of the obnoxious ensigns. He ignored them for five days, but the next day he admitted the Jews to hear their complaint. He had them surrounded with soldiers and threatened them with instant death unless they ceased to trouble him with the matter. The Jews then threw themselves to the ground and bared their necks, declaring that they preferred death to the violation of their laws. Pilate, unwilling to kill so many, succumbed and removed the ensigns.[7]

In the second incident, Pilate used Temple tax funds to build an aqueduct: "A crowd came together and clamored against him," but this time Pilate responded to the nonviolent protest with immediate violence: "He had caused soldiers dressed as civilians to mingle with the multitude, and at a given signal they fell upon the rioters and beat them."[8]

During this same period a band of particularly violent Jews operated to eliminate Roman collaborators, using the same techniques Pilate had used to end the aqueduct protest. The Sicari'i, or "knife men," assassinated those believed dangerous to the freedom fighters' efforts. They generated fear among Jewish collaborators and Romans by slipping in and out of crowds and knifing the targeted individuals, often during daytime gatherings. One revolt of particular note occurred in the year 6 CE. It was led by Judas the Galilean, a man many believed to be the long-hoped-for Messiah. The revolt ended badly for the Jewish rebels, with the crucifixion of about two thousand Jewish men. Tensions continued to rise through the decades of the first century CE until the first major revolution broke out in 66 CE. After four brutal years of warfare, the Romans succeeded in crushing the revolt in 70 CE. The victorious Romans drove home their triumph by destroying the Jewish Temple in Jerusalem and banishing Jews from the city. Jewish hopes for freedom were not extinguished, however, and unrest continued until a second major revolution, led once again by a man believed by most Jews to be the long-awaited Messiah, broke out in 132 CE. This revolt was also crushed, even more violently than the first. The Romans destroyed Jerusalem, rebuilt it in the Roman style, and gave it a Roman name. The Jewish people were banished from the Promised Land for centuries to come.

In the nearly eighteen centuries that passed between the expulsion of the Jews by the Romans and their return with the establishment of Israel as a Jewish nation by the United Nations in May of 1948, Jews were rarely the instigators of significant organized acts of violence in the name of their God. During the Diaspora, if violence occurred in relation to the Jewish people, it more often than not was committed by others against the Jews. There are records of small-scale violence led by Jews but no major acts of violence initiated by the Jewish people; all of that changed with the declaration of Israel's independence in the twentieth century. On May 17, 1948, the day after the U.N. declaration of independence for the state of Israel, Jordanian forces attacked, and violence between Israel and its neighbors has continued to the present day.

As we survey the long history of Judaism, a clear pattern emerges. By far the majority of violence instigated by the Jewish people has been motivated by efforts to take and maintain possession of territory that could be designated a Jewish nation. During the many hundreds of years between the start of the Diaspora and establishment of Israel, military actions of the ancient past were downplayed and texts interpreted so as to discourage acts of violence. One example is the way explanations for the origins of Hanukkah, the Festival of Lights that began in commemoration of a miracle associated with the Maccabean Revolt of 167 BCE, have changed over time. Until recent decades, stories about Hanukkah minimized the role of the militant Jews, and the Passover Haggadah (text read during the Passover celebration) often depicted the wicked son as a soldier. This is in stark contrast to a Haggadah published by the Israeli government in 1970 which contained photos from the 1967 war of the devastated enemy Egyptian territory, and described the war as a modern version of the ten plagues visited by God upon the Egyptians during the time of Moses.[9] These examples highlight the way that violence in Judaism's history has been proportional to Israel's status as a nation. This is not to imply that since becoming a nation in 1948 the nonviolent aspects of Judaism have disappeared. One present-day example of Jewish nonviolent activism is the work being done by the U.S.-based Jewish Voice for Peace, which calls for an end to Israeli occupation of lands not part of the original settlement agreement. There are numerous other groups, like the Jewish Alliance for Peace and Justice and the Jewish Peace Lobby.

## BUDDHISM

Students in introductory religious studies courses often have an especially romanticized view of Buddhism. It is commonly assumed that the history of this tradition, with its foundational doctrine of ahimsa (the duty to do no harm to any living being) is free of violence. This idea has even made its way into print. In one book on Buddhism and nonviolence, for example, the editor says that "no major war has ever been fought in the name of Buddhism."[10] It is simply not true that no wars have ever been fought in the name of the Buddha. As we shall see, although "no major war" in *recent* history has been fought solely in the name of Buddhism, Buddhism has played a significant role in many major wars, both past and present. The history of Buddhist violence is especially informative for those seeking to understand the roots of religious violence, given that the teachings of the Buddha codified in the Four

Noble Truths and Eightfold Path contain nothing which supports violence. These most basic of teachings offer clear admonitions that the believer must refrain from destruction of life and cannot make a living from any occupation that causes harm to others. Stories of the life of the Buddha include descriptions of incidents when he intervened in political disputes to prevent bloodshed. There is very little scriptural warrant for violence, and yet Buddhists have in the past and do today go to war in the name of the Buddha.

There are numerous incidents of religious violence recorded in Buddhist scripture and historical records. Even the great Ashoka (269–32 BCE) of India, commonly portrayed in religious studies textbooks to have been the ideal Buddhist king who decreed nonviolence and religious toleration, apparently did not live as is commonly reported. One Buddhist text, the *Ashokavandana*, tells that Ashoka ordered eighteen thousand non-Buddhists executed because of an insult to Buddhism made by one man. He regularly enforced the death penalty for criminals and executed his own wife.[11] This is hardly the enactment of ahimsa.

In China, Buddhist-inspired rebellion occurred at least nine times between 401 and 516 CE. A monk named Fa-ch'ing proclaimed himself the "Buddha of the Greater Vehicle" and led an army of fifty thousand. At the start of the rebellion, during which Buddhist warriors destroyed monasteries and slaughtered many monks and nuns, Fa-ch'ing announced that any combatant who killed the enemy would become an "enlightenment being" instantly.[12]

Warfare between the Buddhist nations of Burma (Myanmar) and Thailand has often been conducted in the context of Buddhist Holy Warfare. One striking example comes from the early twentieth century. The highest ranking Buddhist monk of Thailand gave a public address in 1910 to mark the coronation of King Rama VI. In this speech the monk said the king was an example of highest virtue in his willingness to sacrifice his life for the nation and Buddhism. The leader of Thai Buddhism applauded the king for his efforts to prepare for war (even though the country was then at peace) by establishing an elite military corps and the "Boy Scout movement to foster in boys the warrior spirit." He claimed that these actions were justified because the Buddha had not taught against war, only the form of "militarism . . . which causes men to kill from sheer blood-lust."[13] Killing is not wrong in war unless it is done for its own sake, according to this interpretation.

Zen Buddhist complicity in the Japanese war effort of World War II has been brilliantly spelled out by Sōtō Zen priest and scholar Brian Daizen Victoria. In *Zen at War* Victoria shows how the relationship between Buddhist monks and governing authorities evolved over 1,500 years into a system of mutual support.[14] In exchange for imperial protection and patronage monks served the state in an arrangement that over time came to be known as "Nation Protecting-Buddhism."[15] The major sects of Zen Buddhism in the country made significant spiritual and material contributions to the war effort. One major sect raised funds to finance the construction of aircraft. Priests conducted special services aimed at generating karmic merit that was believed transferable to soldiers in order to help them realize military victory. Zen priests trained soldiers and factory workers ("Industrial warriors") in the practice of *zazen*, or sitting meditation, a practice originally intended as the path to enlightenment. This form of meditation had long been practiced by Samurai warriors as a means of sharpening the senses and concentration so as to be undistracted in battle. As described in the Bushido warrior text the *Hagakure*, the warrior meditated daily on death in order to purify his mind of selfish desires and make unquestioning obedience to his rulers possible:

> Meditation on inevitable death should be performed daily. Every day when one's body and mind are at peace, one should meditate upon being ripped apart by arrows, rifles, spears, and swords . . . dying of disease or committing seppuku [ritual suicide] at the death of one's master. And every day without fail one should consider himself as dead.[16]

This way of thinking was a powerful tool for strengthening the *kamikaze* ("divine wind") pilots' suicidal resolve as they flew planes into the decks of enemy ships in hopes of winning what Zen leaders called the Holy War: "The source of the spirit of the Special Attack Forces lies in the denial of the individual self and the rebirth of the soul."[17]

In 2001, leaders of two main branches of the Rinzai Zen sect issued public confessions of wrongdoing and awareness that cooperation in the war effort was a betrayal of the Buddha's teachings. Even so, the interplay of Buddhism and violence continues today in other parts of the world.

Armed aggression involving Buddhists has been ongoing for the past twenty years in Sri Lanka as the minority Hindu Tamil and Sinhala-Buddhist majority fight for control of the country. Tens of thousands have died and millions have been displaced in this ethnic conflict. Buddhist monks have played a prominent role in justifying the violence and use ancient Buddhist scriptures and teachings, particularly the *Mahavamsa* (Great Chronicle), to do so.

The *Mahavamsa* is an ancient text written by Sri Lankan Buddhist monks. It serves today as a national chronicle used to support the constitutional favoring of Buddhism and to justify acts of violence against the Hindu Tamil. According to interpreters today, the story it tells (of the Buddha's mystical flight to Sri Lanka during his life and of his deathbed act of entrusting the island to the king of all the gods) is justification of preferential treatment for Buddhists.[18] Other stories in the Chronicle help to justify violence. One especially useful story tells of an ancient war against Hindus conducted by the

Buddhist King Dutthagami (ruler from 101 to 77 BCE). Dutthagami led his troops into battle with a relic of the Buddha as his banner and with monks at his side. The battle was so bloody that at its end the king felt deep sadness for the loss of thousands of lives. His advisors, eight monks, comforted him by explaining that, since the dead were Hindus, "only one and a half humans perished." The rest of the dead were said to be "unbelievers and men of evil life."[19] The idea that the ends justify the means is found frequently in both scripture and tradition. Over the last two decades, as warfare in Sri Lanka rages on, alcoholism, murder, and suicide rates have risen quite dramatically. Sectarian bloodshed has become so common that the chief monk at one major pilgrimage site now carries a handgun.[20] All of this is in stark contrast to the teachings of the great twenty-first-century Buddhist advocates for peace like Thich Nhat Hanh, a Vietnamese Zen Buddhist monk, and Nobel Peace Prize winners, Tenzin Gyatso (His Holiness the Dalai Lama, 1989) and Burmese nonviolent human rights activist Aung San Suu Kyi (1991).

## CHRISTIANITY

The violent history of Christianity is at least as ironic as in Buddhism, given its origins among followers of Jesus of Nazareth, a Jewish man who refused to use force in self-defense and preached a message of nonviolent creative resistance to Roman oppression.[21] As mentioned in the discussion of Judaism above, during Jesus' lifetime, there do seem to have been a few successful nonviolent acts of Jewish resistance to Roman abuses, but we have no evidence tying Jesus' earliest Jewish followers directly to those movements. Given the small geographic area of ancient Palestine, it is quite likely that these nonviolent efforts were known to the early followers of Jesus. Historical evidence clearly indicates that, for the first three centuries, Christians followed the nonviolent example of Jesus, the "Prince of Peace," but that changed rapidly once Christianity transitioned from persecuted minority to privileged majority.

The second century anti-Christian Greek philosopher Celsus was critical of Christians for refusing military service. The historical record shows that at least some of the formal Roman imperial persecutions were in part motivated by the problems raised for the empire by this refusal. In 295 CE, for example, a Christian named Maximilian was called for military service and executed when he openly proclaimed, "I cannot serve as a soldier; I cannot do evil; I am a Christian."[22] From the religion's origins to the early fourth century we find no Christian writer who approved of participation in warfare.[23]

The situation changed dramatically with the rise of Constantine to the throne in the early fourth century. In 313 CE Constantine extended the toleration for Christians earlier proclaimed by Emperor Galerius to include other religions. He gave preferential status to Christians by ordering that property confiscated from them in previous persecutions be returned. Although he did not make it the official religion of the empire, Constantine did make Christianity the fashionable religion when he began practicing it himself. The emperor was not baptized until he was on his deathbed, which seems to indicate that he understood his role as commander-in-chief to be in conflict with the way a baptized Christian was expected to live. (It was not uncommon during the early centuries for powerful men to delay baptism since they believed that killing others was a sin that would lead to damnation. Committing these sins before baptism was acceptable since all guilt for sin was thought to be washed away in the process; committing these sins after baptism was unredeemable.) The Emperor Constantine's actions produced the so-called Constantinian Shift which eventuated in a reversal of attitudes toward military service and participation in war. This reversal was ensured when in 391 CE Emperor Theodosius made Christianity the official state religion and outlawed other forms of worship.

By the early fifth century, violence was no longer strictly forbidden for Christians. The once-persecuted Christians had turned the tables and begun persecuting groups that deviated from the new orthodoxy. Augustine of Hippo (354–430 CE) argued that the empire was just in using violence against the Donatists, a schismatic group in his region of North Africa. The Donatists first arose in response to theological problems raised by bishops and priests who had turned over scriptures for destruction during the last great persecution of Christians under Emperor Diocletian in 303–305 CE. Donatists believed that these clergy were traitors and, as such, had lost their authority to perform the sacraments. Any ordinations performed by them were invalid. By Augustine's time, Donatists in North Africa had begun to use force to prevent their members from returning to nonschismatic churches. It was in response to this threat to Christianity that Augustine first spoke of war as a just endeavor. He wrote that use of violence is just under certain conditions. It must be done to establish peace, be led by proper authorities, and (even in the midst of slaughter!) with the motive of love.[24] He argued that, contrary to the long-standing tradition of nonviolence, military service is not in and of itself wrong for Christians; the problem for Christians is the malice and desire for revenge that accompany much military activity. Augustine's contemporary, Isidore of Pelsium, argued in a similar vein that "private murders are impure and guilty. But there is no guilt in killing in a just war."[25] This line of reasoning led to another reversal. The shift in attitudes initiated by Constantine's ascendancy to power in the fourth century brought about such a change that, by 436 CE, military service was open *only to Christians*.[26] In the space of just four hundred years Christians had left behind their nonviolent origins.

In medieval Europe Christian practice had become so distanced from its nonviolent roots that warriors were ordained as knights in ceremonies called the "eighth sacrament." After formal confession of sins to a priest, the aspirant for knighthood took a purification bath, dressed in white linen garments, and stood an "armed vigil." During the night-long vigil, the candidate left his sword on the altar as he meditated on the vows he would soon take. In the morning, a priest prayed for God's blessing and celebrated the Eucharist while each piece of the initiate's armor and weaponry was blessed and anointed.[27]

In the eight and ninth centuries popes promised eternal life to all who fought to defend the church against Arab or Viking invaders. Over the course of the eleventh century, papal blessing of violence became commonplace. In the mid-eleventh century Pope Leo IX (1049–1054 CE; known mostly for excommunicating the Patriarch of Constantinople in what became the East-West Schism dividing the Church into Roman Catholic and Eastern Orthodox) proclaimed freedom from penalty for sins to warriors fighting the Normans in Italy. Pope Alexander II (1061–1073 CE) granted remission of sin to French knights who fought against the Moors in Spain. In 1074 Gregory VII (1073–85 CE) attempted to establish a knighthood solely dedicated to service of the Church and called for an armed response to defend Constantinople from invasion by "a pagan race." He was unable to carry out his plans due to more pressing problems at home, but Gregory had prepared to personally lead an army of fifty thousand soldiers in holy warfare. Pope Urban II, in November of 1095, proclaimed complete remission of the penalty for all sins to any who joined in what was to become known as the First Crusade against Muslims in Palestine.

Historians debate the definition and causes of the Crusades, but suffice it to say that the endeavor known as the First Crusade marked a "quantum leap" from holy warfare to an ideological synthesis of violence and pilgrimage. Later popes took advantage of this new form of Christian devotional practice—"taking the cross to engage in penitential warfare on behalf of Christ"—and before long crusades were called to combat schematics and heretics in addition to nonbelievers.[28]

The idea of knighthood as service to God was further elaborated in the twelfth century with creation of the Knights Templar. Abbott Bernard of Clairvaux authored a Rule of Life for the Templars and a pamphlet used to attract new recruits. According to the pamphlet, *De Laude Novae Militae*, the knights were ministers of God's justice charged with *malecide*—killing of evil: "'The soldiers of Christ . . . can fight the Lord's battles in all safety. For whether they kill the enemy or die themselves, they need fear nothing. To die for Christ and to kill his enemies, there is no crime in that, only glory.'"[29]

By the sixteenth-century Reformation, Christian acceptance of violence as a means for enforcing compliance to doctrine had become widespread. Religion and politics in Europe were so entwined that it is often difficult to separate out causative factors for wars conducted during this period. In the fifteenth and sixteenth centuries, the sale of indulgences (remission of sin) was a key point in the preaching of crusades against the Turks. Although most associate Martin Luther's (1483–1546) Ninety-five Theses ("Disputation on the Power and Efficacy of Indulgences" used to finance the building of St. Peter's basilica in Rome) with objections to the marketing of salvation, there were earlier attempts at reform of the church's selling indulgences to finance warfare. In the early fifteenth century, Jan Hus (1370–1415) preached against indulgences offered for participation in a crusade against the king of Naples and was as a result executed for heresy. Luther's contemporary, Erasmus, was critical of Pope Leo X's crusades against family enemies.

There were many dissident voices during this time, including those who founded the "Peace Churches" like the Quakers and the Brethren, but the mainstream continued to accept violence as a legitimate Christian response to worldly problems. This acceptance eventuated in all-out warfare between Catholics and Protestants in the early seventeenth century. The Thirty Years War (1618–1648), one of the bloodiest periods in European history, resulted in widespread devastation, with a death toll of millions, killing as much as 30 to 50 percent of the population in some regions. This was an international conflict, but the majority of the fighting took place on German soil. The provisions of the Treaty of Westphalia at the end of the war included, among other things, the stipulation that German princes could dictate the religion of their regions.

Although the Thirty Years War brought about an end to organized Christian-against-Christian violence on a grand scale, it did not end the use of violence by Christians in the service of their God. Theological justification of violence continued with the slave traders and colonialist expansion of Europeans into Africa and the Americas. And it continues to this day, with extremist interpretations of the scriptures, preaching in churches aimed at support of a war that has been incorrectly framed in terms of Christian versus Muslim, and isolated acts of violence by individuals against people like abortion clinic employees and homosexual individuals. Some conservative groups believe that Christ's Second Coming will not happen until Israel is solidly in the hands of the Jewish people. These so-called Christian Zionists see the current U.S.-Iraq War as one piece of the Divine Plan for eventual Christian world domination.[30] A 2002 survey published by CommonDream.org showed that evangelical Christians were the biggest supporters of the U.S. military attacks on Iraq and of support for Israel against the Palestinians.[31]

## ISLAM

Islam is the newest of the religions covered here. It arose in the early seventh century on the Arabian Peninsula out of a polytheistic nomadic culture and has spread rapidly across the world since that time. A basic tenet of Islam is that the revelation received by Muhammad from God is the final revelation, the last in a long line of prophecy that began with Adam, continued on through the Jewish prophets and Jesus, until its culmination in Muhammad. According to Islam, the Jews and Christians misunderstood God's intent: the Jews by failure to missionize because they narrowly interpreted the covenant as applying only to the Jews, and the Christians by claiming Jesus was the divine incarnate. In Muhammad's life and in the holy book of Islam, the Quran, an accurate presentation of God's will has been preserved. God's will is absolute in Islam, and so there is no distinction between religious and secular for many Muslims. This is why in some countries today, like Nigeria and Pakistan, the Quran is considered to be equivalent to, or the basis of, the national constitution.

The history of the faith, like the others we have examined here, contains a great deal of violence. Sadly, Islam is currently more "infamous" for its violent history than other faiths because of recent episodes of very public violence committed in the name of Allah (literally, "the God"). Nonviolence is not often associated with Islam even though it began with the peaceful preaching of a simple message that God is one. In recent times, Islam has spread across Southeast Asia and Africa without warfare, but beginning in 622 CE, Year One of the Muslim calendar, the faith's history is colored by acts of aggression.[32]

Jihad is the term most commonly associated in the Western mind with the subject of Islam and violence. Literally translated the term means struggle, striving, exertion—not "holy war" as is sometimes claimed. In the Hadith literature, collections of sayings and accounts of Muhammad's life, jihad takes different forms, classified as the Greater and Lesser Jihad. The Greater Jihad is the inner struggle of the believer to overcome our own interior tendencies to do evil, and the Lesser Jihad encompasses all activities to combat social injustice. Obviously, the Greater Jihad is conducted nonviolently, but in the lesser forms, jihad can be unarmed or armed efforts to establish justice. Since

Allah decrees in the Quran that the Prophet Muhammad is the example to be followed, and since Muhammad engaged in armed conflict, the traditional interpretation is that God permits, and may even require, Muslims to use violence under certain circumstances.[33]

Even though much has been made of the fact that jihad does not necessarily mean "Holy War," the truth remains that the classical Muslim understanding was apparently just that—jihad meant "warfare with spiritual significance." Its standard definition in terms of Muslim law today is that given in the *Encyclopedia of Islam*: "'In law, according to general doctrine and in historical tradition, the *jihad* consists of military action with the object of the expansion of Islam and, if need be, of its defense.'"[34]

Muhammad personally participated in at least twenty-seven military battles and sanctioned about fifty-nine others. The Quran itself valorizes these battles: in Sura 8, for example, we read that God instigated the battle of Badr in 624 CE and sent angels to ensure victory. In the decades after the Prophet's death in 632 CE, there was conflict within the Muslim community over the issue of leadership, and sects soon formed. Clearly the Lesser Jihad was central to the development of the faith.

A particularly violent sect developed in the eighth century out of the Ismailis, an offshoot of the Shi'ite tradition. The Shi'ites separated from the mainstream over the question of leadership. They believed that leadership of the faith could only be in the hands of Muhammad's cousin and son-in-law, and lineage should flow through his blood relations since they were thought to share in the spiritual power of the Prophet. Ismaili Shi'ites were extremist militants who used murder in a systematic way to further political goals. The Ismaili were a messianic movement who believed that their founding leader, Isma'il, was the immortal Mahdi, the Islamic messiah who would not die until he had conquered the entire world.[35]

The group first came to the attention of European society as a result of the Christian Crusades. Among the earliest descriptions of the sect is this late twelfth-century note by the Christian Archbishop of Tyre:

> There is, in the province of Tyre . . . a people who possess ten strong castles. . . . The bond of submission and obedience that binds this people to their Chief is so strong that there is no task so arduous, difficult, or dangerous that any one of them would not undertake to perform it with the greatest zeal, as soon as the Chief commanded it. If, for example, there be a prince who is hated or mistrusted by this people, the Chief gives a dagger to one or more of his followers. At once whoever receives the command sets out on his mission, without considering the consequences of the deed. . . . Both our people and the Saracens call them Assissini; we do not know the origin of this name.[36]

ne Assassins, an elite Ismaili military unit, seem to have come into being at the end of the eleventh century after the sect had been targeted by the dominant Sunni military forces. Little is known about the inner operations of the group; it was a secret society that guarded knowledge through a hierarchical system involving initiation and oaths. They conducted a "war of terror" against kings, princes, and holy men who condemned the sect. Within the Ismaili, the Assassins were believed to be among the most faithful of Muslims. As such, they earned the ultimate prize—immediate entry into Paradise upon death.[37]

In Islam, as in the other religions we have surveyed here, there is a nonviolent strain of thought, and for the majority of Muslims today, violence has not been a part of their self-understanding. The Quran, like other scriptures, contains admonitions to peaceful coexistence. For example, Sura 2 says, "Let there be no compulsion in religion," and Sura 67, "What army can help you apart from the Beneficent (God)?" In the Sufi tradition of Islam, mystics have often written against violence. The Sri Lankan Sufi master Bawa Muhaiyadeen has written that "it is compassion that conquers. It is unity that conquers. . . . The sword does not conquer; love is sharper than the sword."[38] One particularly strong and eloquent voice for nonviolence in Islam today comes from Turkey in a movement shaped by Sufism. Said Nursi (1877–1960) and Fethullah Gülen (1941–) have been tremendously influential in contemporary Turkey as peace activists. Both men were shaped by firsthand experience with the devastation of violence, Nursi as a soldier and prisoner of war during World War I and Gülen as an activist during the violence between Turkish leftists and nationalists in the 1960s and 1970s.

Nursi called his nonviolent activism *musbet hareket*, which means "positive action" and goes beyond mere pacifism. He eschewed politics in favor of preaching and teaching because he saw how dangerous the pull of political power can be; in one of his most famous sayings, he once declared, "I take refuge in God from Satan and politics." He insisted that the Quran does not allow "ends justify the means" thinking and was successful in defusing plans for revolution on at least one occasion by convincing Kurdish tribal leaders that their planned violent rebellion against the Turkish secular government would bring further injustice.[39]

Fethullah Gülen is an influential preacher and teacher of Islamic thought who has dedicated his most recent efforts to establishing schools and advocating for interreligious tolerance. He has met with many leaders of the world's religions, including Pope John Paul II, the Chief Rabbi of Israel, and the Ecumenical Patriarch of Constantinople, in order to enhance communication and cooperation among religions. The efforts of his followers have brought Gülen's theology of activism for tolerance and peace to the attention of Western scholars. In 2005, the journal *The Muslim World* devoted an entire issue to his impact on Islam in Turkey, and Rice University hosted the conference "Islam in the Contemporary World: The Fethullah Gülen Movement in Thought and Practice." The Movement has established hundreds of schools in numerous countries, the Turkish Teacher's Foundation, the Journalists' and Writers' Foundation which brings Muslims and secularists into dialogue, a newspaper, a television and radio station, and a bank which operates according to the Quranic prohibition against charging interest. In Gülen's reading, the Quran is a text of tolerance and compassion and Islam is a religion of mercy. "A real Muslim, one who understands Islam in every aspect, cannot be a terrorist. . . . Religion does not approve of the killing of people in order to attain a goal."[40]

It is an unfortunate truth that no purely nonviolent religious tradition has been sustained long enough in human history to become a major player on the world stage. Even practitioners of Jainism, wherein *ahimsa* is the central ethical principle (so much so that monks and nuns often wear masks over their faces and sweep the ground in front of them as they walk to avoid killing even a gnat or ant) have found justification for participation in warfare. Jain political teachings are similar to the Hindu in that the Jain king was responsible for ensuring the safety of the community, and a warrior class evolved to assist the king in carrying out this function.[41]

This brief survey reveals that violence has been justified by members of religions even if the scriptures provide little or no warrant for it, and nonviolence has arisen in religious traditions that seem to have their foundations in violent acts. What is it about human beings that makes it possible for us to justify horrendous acts in the name of love? And just what is it about religion that makes human beings feel compelled to engage in violence for the sake of it?

## NOTES

1. *Bhagavad Gita*, trans. Barbara Stoler Miller (New York: Bantam Books, 1986), 3.35. Citations hereafter in the text will be abbreviated BG followed by chapter and verse numbers.

2. Brian K. Smith, "Hinduism," in *God's Rule: The Politics of World Religions*, ed. Jacob Neusner (Washington, DC: Georgetown University Press, 2003), 185–212.

3. *Artha Shastra* 18.21ff; quoted in Smith, "Hinduism," 191.

4. Mohandas K. Gandhi, *The Teaching of the Gita* (Bombay: Bharatiya Vidya Bhavan, 1971), 4–6.

5. Jyotirmaya Sharma, *Hindutva: Exploring the Idea of Hindu Nationalism* (New Delhi, India: Penguin Books India, 2003).

6. K. Lawson Younger Jr., "The Deportations of the Israelites," *Journal of Biblical Literature* 117, no. 2 (Summer 1998): 201–28. See also Michael Astour, "841 B.C.: The First Assyrian Invasion of Israel," *Journal of the American Oriental Society* 91, no. 3 (July–September 1971): 383–89.

7. Josephus, *The New Complete Works of Josephus*, trans. William Whiston (Grand Rapids, MI: Kregel Academic & Professional, 1999) (*War* 2:175–203; *Antiquities* 18:55–59).

8. Josephus, *New Complete Works* (*Antiquities* 18:60–62; *War* 2:175–177).

9. Jeremy Milgrom, "'Let Your Love for Me Vanquish Your Hatred for Him': Nonviolence and Modern Judaism," in *Subverting Hatred: The Challenge of Nonviolence in Religious Traditions*, ed. Daniel L. Smith-Christopher (Maryknoll, NY: Orbis Books, 1998), 130.

10. Kenneth Kraft, ed., *Inner Peace, World Peace: Essays on Buddhism and Nonviolence* (New York: SUNY Press, 1992), 1.

11. Brian Daizen Victoria, *Zen at War* (Lanham, MD: Rowman & Littlefield, 1997/2006), 197–98.

12. Jacques Gernet, *Buddhism in Chinese Society: An Economic History from the Fifth to the Tenth Century*, trans. F. Verellen (New York: Columbia University Press, 1998), 287–88. See also John Ferguson, *War and Peace in the World's Religions* (New York: Oxford University Press, 1978), 52.

13. Trevor Ling, *Buddhism, Imperialism, and War* (London: George Allen & Unwin, 1979), 136ff.

14. For an in-depth history of Japanese Buddhist warrior monks from the sixth through the fourteenth centuries, see Mikael S. Adolphson, *The Teeth and Claws of the Buddha: Monastic Warriors and Sōhei in Japanese History* (Honolulu: University of Hawaii Press, 2007).

15. Victoria, *Zen at War*, 200.

16. Victoria, *Zen at War*, 220.

17. Dr. Masunaga Reiho quoted in Victoria, *Zen at War*, 139.

18. Richard Gombrich, "Is the Sri Lankan War a Buddhist Fundamentalism?" in *Buddhism, Conflict and Violence in Modern Sri Lanka*, ed. Mahinda Deegalle (London: Routledge, 2006), 22–37.

19. *Mahavamsa* 25:101–11, cited in Stanley J. Tambiah, *Buddhism Betrayed: Religion, Politics, and Violence in Sri Lanka* (Chicago: University of Chicago Press, 1992), 1.

20. Gananath Obeyesekere, "Buddhism, Ethnicity, and Identity: A Problem in Buddhist History," in *Buddhism: Conflict and Violence in Modern Sri Lanka*, ed. Mahinda Deegalle (London: Routledge, 2006), 134–62.

21. Walter Wink, *Jesus and Nonviolence: A Third Way* (Minneapolis: Augsburg Fortress, 2003).

22. James F. Childress, "Moral Discourse about War in the Early Church," *Journal of Religious Ethics* 12, no. 1 (January 2006): 2–18.

23. Childress, "Moral Discourse."

24. Roland H. Bainton, *Christian Attitudes toward War and Peace* (Nashville: Abingdon Press, 1960), 91–93.

25. Childress, "Moral Discourse," 5, 14.

26. John Howard Yoder, "The Constantinian Sources of Western Social Ethics," in *The Priestly Kingdom: Social Ethics as Gospel* (Notre Dame, IN: University of Notre Dame Press, 1984), 125–47.

27. James A. Aho, *Religious Mythology and the Art of War: Comparative Religious Symbolisms of Military Violence*, vol. 3, Contributions to the Study of Religion, ed. Henry W. Bowden (Westport, CT: Greenwood Press, 1981), 81–85.

28. Norman Housley, *Contesting the Crusades* (Malden, MA: Blackwell Publishing, 2006), 1–10.

29. Aho, *Religious Mythology*, 84.

30. See, for example, Michael Evans, *Beyond Iraq: The Next Move—Ancient Prophecy and Modern-Day Conspiracy Collide* (Lakeland, FL: White Stone Books, 2003).

31. Jim Lobe, "Conservative Christians Biggest Backers of Iraq War," Common-Dreams.org, October 12, 2002, www.commondreams.org/headlines02/1010-02.htm (accessed January 3, 2008).

32. Rabia Terri Harris, "Nonviolence in Islam: The Alternative Community Tradition," in *Subverting Hatred: The Challenge of Nonviolence in Religious Traditions*, ed. Daniel L. Smith-Christopher (Maryknoll, NY: Orbis Books, 1998), 95.

33. Harris, "Nonviolence in Islam," 96.

34. David Cook, *Understanding Jihad* (Berkeley: University of California Press, 2005), 2.

35. Abdulaziz Abdulhussein Sachedina, *Islamic Messianism: The Idea of the Mahdi in Twelver Shi`ism* (Albany, NY: SUNY Press, 1981), 13.

36. Bernard Lewis, *The Assassins: A Radical Sect in Islam* (New York: Basic Books, 1968/2002), 3–4.

37. Lewis, *The Assassins*, 45–47.

38. Quoted in Harris, "Nonviolence in Islam," 111.

39. Zeki Saritoprak," An Islamic Approach to Peace and Nonviolence: A Turkish Experience," *Muslim World* 95 (July 2005): 413–27.

40. M. Fethullah Gülen, *Toward a Global Civilization of Love and Tolerance* (Somerset, NJ: The Light, 2006), 187.

41. Paul Dundas, *The Jains* (London: Routledge, 1992), 102.

## Chapter Three

# Searching for the Roots of "Religious" Violence

The proliferation of media and scholarly attention focused on religion in recent decades is striking, given that for most of the last century the prevailing academic opinion was that religion had become irrelevant to understanding Western society. Sigmund Freud's view that religion is a neurosis rooted in infantile wishes for protection which must be abandoned in favor of science was an early expression of what became the dominant social scientific stance on religion in the twentieth century.[1] The belief was that modernity and secularization would lead to the end of religion as a significant force in human life. For example, before September 11, 2001, most academic writings on terrorism either ignored religion or treated it as a minor factor. This was the case in spite of the fact that a disproportionate number of terrorist acts since 1980 have been committed by groups claiming religious motivation.

Rather than bringing about the end of religion, it now appears that modernization has led to its rebirth as a major social and political force.[2] This realization has begun to make its way into the academic world, and theories about the role of religion in bringing about violence have exploded in the literature. Once considered of no consequence in its own right, the tide of opinion about religion has turned so radically that sometimes one gets the impression that religion and only religion must be the cause of all violence. Sociologist Peter Berger, for example, was once a leading proponent of the secularization thesis but has come to understand the issues differently in recent years. Berger now sees that the relationship between religion and modernization is quite a bit more complex. He notes that, in reality, rather than dying off, religious institutions have flourished almost in direct proportion to the extent that they have *not* adapted to the modern world.[3] Counterintuitively, the less religious ideologies change, the stronger they seem to be in today's world.

33

The discipline-specific focus that is characteristic of the academic world combined with this newfound enthusiasm to place religion at the center of the conversation has resulted in a dizzying array of claims. Scholars have identified the roots of religious violence in nearly every aspect of human life. In this intriguing reversal, politics, secularization and modernization, economics and environmental resource scarcity, the type of God-image a group accepts (especially the belief in one God), the sacred writings of religious traditions, human psychology, and even the biological evolution of human beings are all set forth as causative factors. While this multiplicity of explanations is to some extent a by-product of the academic context in which theorizing takes place, it is also a reflection of the complexity of human behavior. How are we to make sense of all of these claims without falling prey to the temptation of reifying religion and making it the scapegoat?

As a step toward developing a more balanced understanding of the problem, in this chapter we will survey a representative sample of explanations. We will mine them as we go, looking for materials out of which to construct a new model that acknowledges the complex interplay of religion with myriad aspects of life and at the same time illuminates the deeper facets of personal accountability.

## RELIGIOUS VIOLENCE, BIOLOGY, AND GROUP SELECTION

Evolutionary scientists tend to see religion (and all human endeavors) as an outgrowth of the evolutionary process, a kind of adaptation, either at the level of the individual or group. Biologist Richard Dawkins says all religion is a "virus of the mind"[4] that causes pernicious delusions of gods which ensure survival not of the human but of the idea. Dawkins equates all religion with its most exclusivist forms and concludes that it has virtually no redeeming value.[5] Cognitive anthropologist Pascal Boyer argues that "religious concepts are parasitic upon intuitive ontology" and are a side effect of the type of brain humans have evolved.[6] In a similar vein, cognitive psychologist/anthropologist Scott Atran argues that religions are tremendously costly (read violent), counterintuitive, and counterfactual constructs that have no evolutionary adaptive value. They developed as by-products of cognitive structures that do enhance survival but are themselves not adaptive.[7]

Group selection models of evolution more directly address religion's relation to violence and tend to see religion more positively. According to group selectionists, helping behaviors evolve in order to enhance the survival of the group. Religions, with their admonitions to care for those in need, are one form of helping behavior. One way religion may have evolved is as a sort of "pseudo-kinship" that worked to trick the brain into substituting shared beliefs for shared genes. For group selectionists, although religion once served to enhance survival in small societies of interrelated people, today it has become irrelevant at best, dangerous at worst. The problem is that "group selection favors within group niceness and between group nastiness." Interactions between groups "may exhibit the rudiments of moral conduct but are dominated by exploitation on all sides."[8] Religion is maladaptive in today's "multiracial, multicreedal world" because of the tendency to insist on exclusive claims to truth which lead to violence.[9] These theories are controversial and have been questioned at many levels. Holmes Ralston III, a philosopher of biology, for example, challenges these theorists to explain the missionary impulse to convert outsiders if religion's evolutionary function is to foster group loyalty.[10]

An in-depth response to evolutionary views of religion and violence is beyond the scope of this project, but many aspects of human existence indicate that appeal to genetic survival urges is too reductionist to be of much use in the long run. While evolutionary biopsychology may illuminate the deepest roots of violence, it is not very useful in explaining many aspects of human behavior. Kinship and group selection models are undercut, for example, by the fact that humans have often gone to war against their "own kind." The American Civil War is a case-in-point: brothers fought against brothers in the name of ideological differences. How does it happen that pseudo-kinship constructs override biology? Our development as a species is a dual process of biological and cultural evolution. The human mind is a hybrid outcome of biology and culture. What may be most distinctive about us in comparison to other creatures are behaviors and characteristics that arise out of our cultures. Our particular need for interpersonal relatedness, arising as it does out of biological and cultural influences, gives rise to complex collective endeavors like religions. That which makes us truly unique, then, seems to be more historical and ontogenetic than biological.[11]

Further, if the biological views are correct, we have virtually no agency to effect lasting change. If we accept the claims that "it's all in the genes," amelioration of the problem of religious violence in the near future is not feasible, and despair in the short term seems the only reasonable response. For most of us, this interpretation is excessively fatalistic and depressing. We ought not, indeed cannot, abdicate all responsibility in favor of the process of genetic evolution. In truth, the most compelling theories about the origins of religious violence are tied to social and cultural factors which might be considered epiphenomena in relation to biological realities.

## SECULARIZATION AND MODERNIZATION

We have seen that modernization and secularization may well have the counterintuitive effect of strengthening traditional religious ideologies. Now analysts are so accepting of this once-denied relationship that the spread of secular Western values is today acknowledged as a major cause of religious violence. It is assumed by many that the clash of conservative religious worldviews with Western liberal attitudes toward women's roles, sexuality, and capitalism inevitably leads to violence. This interpretation has become commonplace since the attacks in the United States by Al-Qaeda members on September 11, 2001.

We often see the phenomenon of secularization combined with globalization when offered as the primary reason for the recent upsurge in violence associated with religious ideologies. Most simply defined, globalization is the production and trading of goods internationally, but in the context of understanding religious violence, the added dimension of social change stimulated by increased contact among cultures must be considered as well. Here we will focus primarily on the social dimensions of secularization and globalization.

### Globalization and Violence

Although globalization and secularization are seen by many to go hand-in-hand, for our purposes it will be helpful to begin by attempting to address the two issues separately. The globalization trend has been intensely debated in recent decades: is it a good or bad phenomenon? Depending upon one's perspective, it is either the positive integration of economic, political, and cultural systems across the globe, or the imperialist Americanization and domination of the world by the United States. Some say it is a positive force for economic growth and democratic freedom, while others say it is a means of exploitation and suppression of human rights that results in destruction of the environment.

Increases in trade, investment, and migration have occurred so rapidly and on such a large scale in recent years that the world seems to have been radically and permanently transformed. Since 1950, for example, the volume of world trade increased twenty-fold. Since World War II many governments have adopted free-market economic systems and established international agreements to promote trade and investment. American and European corporations have built factories in poorer nations the world over and created an international industrial-financial business structure. Advances in information and communications technologies have spectacularly transformed life in many areas of the world. Fans of globalization claim that the process allows poor countries and their citizens to raise their standards of living, while opponents of it assert that the creation of an unfettered international free market has benefited Western multinational corporations to the detriment of local cultures and people. Resistance to globalization has arisen at popular and governmental levels as people and governments try to negotiate the changes brought by globalization.[12]

One very important negative effect of the process has been the development of increased economic inequalities and social unrest. Although studies show that poverty in and of itself is not a direct cause of terrorism, it does seem to be the case that the social inequalities resulting from uneven distribution of the benefits of globalization do matter.[13] The World Bank Development Report of 2001 shows that nearly half of the world's six billion people live on less than two dollars per day, have limited access to health care and education, and have virtually no political power.[14] The politics and economics at work in multinational corporate development and "out-sourcing" have tended to build up metropolitan centers in a way that creates huge disparities in power and development within and between countries. Uneven development within the borders of nations places stress on national identities and communal relations. When community bonds are strained in these ways, people often seek to build new identities by reinforcing ethnic or religious ties.

Another way that globalization has intensified ethno-religious conflict has been a direct result of free trade policies and widespread access to communications and information technologies. Simplified access to sophisticated tools of war and worldwide networking make massively destructive violence an easier option for relatively unsophisticated groups.[15] We will return to the issue of individual identity formation in chapter 4, but for now, it is helpful to note that de-reification of worldviews is happening rapidly as American political, social, and cultural ways flood regions of the world that until recent times have been relatively isolated from the rest of the world. The overwhelming amount of information about alternative worldviews flowing through new communications technologies is creating crises of knowledge and meaning-making in many of these regions.

All of this, combined with concerns that Western social and cultural values are rapidly reconfiguring the extant religious landscape, contributes to the decisions people make to commit acts of violence in the name of religion. In recent years this seems to have become the framework for justification in some Islamic cultures. "They [Westerners] are only after your minerals and want to turn your country into a market for their goods."[16] This statement by Iran's Ayatollah Khomeini sums up the attitude of many who oppose globalization. Although he died in 1989 his writings continue to inspire those Muslims who

see in globalization a threat to their religious way of life. Khomeini's portrayal of Western influence as "satanic" and claims that "the agents of colo-
nialism" intend to bring about a "black and dreadful" future because they see
Islam as "the major obstacle in the path of their materialistic ambitions and
the chief threat to their political power"[17] show the powerful impact on religious thought that the side effects of globalization have had.

## Cultural Secularization

A brief exploration of the work by one prominent scholar of religious violence who sees secularization as a primary cause will suffice here. Mark Jurgensmeyer, currently director of the Orfalea Center for Global and International Studies and professor of sociology and religious studies at the
University of California in Santa Barbara, says that "religion is not innocent"
when it comes to violence, particularly when it fuses with cultural expressions of unrest.[18] He points to comments made by the Israeli mother of a child
who was on a bus bombed by Arab members of Hamas in 1998 as evidence
for his claims that secularization and modernization are to blame. The Israeli
mother expressed anger not at the bombers but against Israel's prime minis-
ter for having negotiated peace agreements with Yasar Arafat. Jurgensmeyer
says that the woman's comments "demonstrated that the religious war in Israel and Palestine has not been a war between religions, but a double set of
wars—Jewish and Muslim—against secularism." He argues that this disillu-
sionment with Western values has led to a "'loss of faith' in the ideological
form of that culture, secular nationalism."[19] "The perception that the modern
idea of secular nationalism was insufficient in moral, political, and social
terms" is central to every conflict he has studied, and so, he argues, "the motivating *cause*—if such a term can be used—was the sense of a loss of identity and control in the modern world."[20] He further claims that "guys throw
bombs" as a reaction to humiliation and emasculation resulting from economic frustrations. Religious ideas add a powerful "symbolic empowerment"
dimension to the violence through which "guys" are able to assert masculinity threatened by the consequences of secularization and modernization.[21] We
will more fully examine the portions of Jurgensmeyer's thesis that address
psychological motivations in more detail shortly, but it suffices for the present to note that although his insights into the role that Cosmic War ideologies
play in fueling violence are very important and he does acknowledge that religion is not the sole cause, this reductionist psychological interpretation is
problematic. Also problematic are aspects of his prescription for curing the
problem of religious violence. In the last chapter of *Terror in the Mind of
God*, Jurgensmeyer outlines several scenarios for the end of terrorism. The

scenarios include the use of legal or military force to subdue or terrify the violent factions into submission, the possibility that terrorism will win out, the separation of religion from politics, or "healing politics with religion."

As for the suggestion that compartmentalization of religion into the private sphere might solve the problem, this idealistic goal rings true at one level, but probably primarily only for those of us whose lives are imbued with Western European or American political ideas. The history of the United States illustrates the impossibility of segregating religion and politics. In the United States separation of church and state is a foundational political tenet. Comparatively speaking, religiously motivated violence is minimal in the country today with diverse religious ideologies coexisting in relative peace. Rodney Stark argues that American religious civility is a product of pluralism: "The key to high levels of local religious commitment *and* of religious civility is not fewer religions, but more."[22] But many argue that what has actually happened in the United States is that America has evolved a distinctive form of civil religion in which references to God are politically acceptable and important aspects of our culture, like the Declaration of Independence and the flag, are imbued with a sacred character. In a sense, we in the United States have not separated religion from politics at all; we've simply developed a new form of religious expression. Religions are meaning-making systems and as such necessarily, for their practitioners, inform politics. As Gandhi insisted, the person who believes that religion and politics have nothing to do with one another quite clearly understands neither religion nor politics. Our discussion of the psychodynamic interplay of the individual and the collective unconscious in the last chapters will shed additional light on the mechanisms at work here.

Jurgensmeyer's last proposed solution, healing politics with religion, also rings true at one level. Violence will end, he says, "when secular authorities embrace moral values, including those associated with religion."[23] His analysis of religious violence is insightful and useful in understanding the broader issues at work. But this recommendation that we must "heal politics with religion" is made without guidance as to how a culture of religious intolerance and fanaticism can be transformed into one of secular government with privatized religion, or how nations are to determine which among the many competing religious moralities they ought to adopt, never mind how a government might go about implementing the healing process. Healing is most certainly the goal, but unless it begins at the level of the individual it simply will not happen. To claim that politics can be healed with religion is to reify politics as well as religion and create an illusory space within which abstract concepts must be thought to act upon one another. As we discovered in our discussion of reification, this sort of talk reinscribes our sense of impotence to effect change since the individual human remains outside the sphere of influence.

Secularization models as a major cause of religious violence may make some sense today, but what about in the past? The Protestant Reformation in sixteenth-century Europe broke up the hegemony of the papacy over Christianity. This disruption of control led to many overtly religious wars throughout Europe, as Catholic Christians struggled for political control over the Protestants, and various forms of Protestantism struggled for control over one another. Every major Reformation movement became embroiled in intense theological and political conflict which led to the "Confessional Era" in which churches developed statements that delineated their beliefs, and princes and clergy required profession of allegiance to them. Widespread devastation due to events like the Wars of Religion and the St. Bartholomew's Day Massacre of August 1572 in France set the stage for secularization in the eighteenth century with the Reign of Terror, when the only form of worship allowed was of the Goddess Reason, and the French Revolution. Post-Reformation confessionalism was closely tied to the evolution of the modern nation-state and led to the Thirty Years War (1618–1648), one of the most devastating conflicts in European history. It is one of history's greatest ironies that religious conflict provided a major stimulus for the process of secularization itself.

The relationship between religion and secularization is complicated even further when we consider two other examples: England and India. In England today, Anglicanism is the official state religion and the monarch is the head of both church and government. And yet, British society is quite secular and the Parliament passes legislation not to conform to dogma of the Church of England but rather from a secular basis. India is quite secular in terms of its governmental structure, but Indian society as a whole tends to be very religious.[24] These examples make it more difficult to draw clear connections between secularization and religious expression.

The secularization/modernization thesis is more directly challenged by Jonathan Fox's empirical analysis of data on ethnic and religious conflict since 1945. Fox, an Israeli political scientist, points out that the majority of scholarship done thus far is either purely theoretical or based on ad hoc analysis. What little empirical research there is has focused very narrowly and so does not lend itself to accurate generalizations about the overall impact of religions on conflict.[25] Fox used data from two major projects: the University of Maryland's Minorities at Risk Project (MAR) and George Mason University's Political Instability Task Force State Failure database. MAR monitors and evaluates conflicts of politically active groups in all countries with populations of five hundred thousand or more, and tracks 284 politically active ethnic groups on political, economic, and cultural dimensions.[26] The Political Instability Task Force (PITF) is a group of scholars and researchers originally brought together in 1994 at the request of senior policy makers in the U.S. government. The State Failure database[27] maintains comparative information on cases of total state failure and periods of political instability between 1955 and 2005, in nations with populations over five hundred thousand.

Fox's analysis of this data shows that, although religion is a contributor, it has not been the sole or even primary causative factor in conflicts since 1945. The *primary* cause of conflict is nationalism in separatist forms. Religion can be used to intensify ethnic conflicts and is increasingly being employed in this way. There is no evidence to support claims that religious objections to secularization are the initial or principal cause of this conflict.[28]

The secondary effects of religious claims on conflict take different forms. Fox found an intriguing and counterintuitive relationship between ethnic protest and religion: "The presence of religious identity and complaints over religious issues in an ethnic conflict make protest less likely. This is exactly the opposite of what we would expect." Religion has little or no impact in ethnic conflicts *unless* it is combined with demands for self-determination.[29] In a 2006 essay, Mark Jurgensmeyer agrees that "religion is not the initial problem, but the fact that religion is the medium through which [alienation, marginalization, and social frustration] are expressed is problematic." This religious "antimodernism" and "antiglobalism" personalizes the tensions, provides an organizational network, provides moral justification for violence, and adds Cosmic Warfare imagery which absolutizes the conflict. In this way religion becomes not the primary cause of religious violence but rather "a problematic partner of political confrontation."[30] Once again, we have a potent analysis of the problem, but we have added new questions. Why is it that religious ideologies only seem to play a role in conflict when combined with nationalism or demands for self-determination? The answer to this question lies in the individual human psyche, a phenomenon we will examine in more depth in the following chapters.

## Politics, Not Religion, as Primary Cause

A number of recent publications examine the question of religious violence in relation to politics and conclude that religion in and of itself does not cause violence. Like Jonathan Fox's work, in these analyses religion is a secondary factor in the generation of bloodshed. These theorists argue that sometimes religious ideals are co-opted as a consequence of the need to rally support for political goals and that sometimes religious rhetoric is deliberately used in order to mask political agendas.

Ram Puniyani, an Indian economist, claims that the majority of violence today is really politics clothed in the language of religion. Pointing to his own country, Puniyani says that religious ideologies are being exploited on a grand scale today by the elite of Indian society. The Hindutva movement, which insists that India must be governed by Hindu religious teachings, makes use of ancient ideologies not to glorify Hinduism but rather to reestablish the political and social power of the upper caste and justify demonization of all non-Hindus.[31] According to Harvard sociologist Stanley Tambiah, "Civilian riots are a mode of conducting politics by other means."[32] Ethno-religious violence in India shows evidence of careful planning and tends to be carried out by people from a wide range of the population with direction from politicians and members of the professional classes. Police are often reported to be complicit either through nonaction or direct participation, as in the Bombay riots of 1992–1993 and the 2002 Hindu-Muslim riots in Ahmedabad, when police fired primarily on the slum areas. "Institutionalized riot systems" have evolved as networks organized by political parties to stage riots against ethnic and religious minority groups.[33]

On the world stage, Puniyani argues, the government of the United States also uses religion to mask its true agenda. The United States has had to find a new enemy since the demise of communism and so has instituted a policy of demonization of Islam in its place. He says this demonization is made necessary because American imperialism requires justification for its military presence all over the world. America maintains military bases in or has troops deployed to at least 144 countries and territories beyond its own borders.[34] The rhetoric of a "war on terror," in other words, disguises the real motives behind troop deployment and invasions by U.S. armed forces in recent years. In order to justify its military presence, which Puniyani perceives to be in the service not of a war on terror but rather of globalization and economic domination, the U.S. government disguises its agenda as religious warfare—Islam versus Christian democracy.

In a similar vein Robert Pape, a University of Chicago political scientist, argues that religion is not the motivating factor behind most suicide bombings:

> Over half of all suicide terrorist attacks, all around the world since 1980, pretty much since they've begun in the modern period, are not associated with Islamic fundamentalism . . . what over 95 percent of all suicide terrorist attacks . . . have in common is not religion but a specific strategic goal: to compel a modern democracy to withdraw combat forces.[35]

In Pape's analysis, terrorism of this sort is primarily about defending territory and culture against invading forces and not about religious fundamentalisms. Pape says that suicide terrorism, in particular, displays a kind of three-fold logic of political, social, and individual strategic value. Typical suicide terrorists are of normal psychology, are better off economically than the norm for their community, are well supported by social networks, and have strong emotional commitments to their national identity. These individuals seem to perceive themselves as acting altruistically for a social group that is dedicated to legitimate goals in the service of political coercion.

Suicide attacks are nearly always a response to foreign occupation but do become more likely when the predominant religion of the occupying forces differs from that of the region under occupation. Religion comes into play after the fact, according to Pape's theory. There are three reasons for this secondary role of religious ideologies: the fear that occupying forces will attempt to force change, often seen to include conversion to the religion of the occupying forces; religion facilitates demonization of the other; and religion transforms suicide (condemned by most religions) into martyrdom.[36]

## RESOURCE SCARCITY

Some theorists believe that religious violence can be explained as a response to restricted access to or insufficient quantities of various intangible resources. Intangible religious resources include ultimate truth, eternal salvation, and sacred spaces. Monotheisms automatically and implicitly create scarce resources by virtue of the fact that the core doctrine insists there is only one true God. An intriguing facet of the impact that globalization has had on religious violence has to do with the creation of "religioscapes," subjective religious maps, and new "moral geographies" that evolve between immigrant and diasporic groups of people.[37] Of special interest to us here are theories that religious people commit acts of violence because religious doctrines themselves, especially monotheisms, create a kind of theological scarcity by making exclusivist claims to salvation.

### Monotheism as Cosmic Resource Scarcity

Scarcity of resources occurs when a society does not have sufficient supplies to produce enough of a specific resource to fulfill particular requirements. Scarcity implies that not all of society's goals can be attained at the same time, so when the resources desired or needed by a society for achieving its goals are not in abundant supply, trade-offs must be made. In human experience, conflict has often been the end result. Land, natural resources, manufactured goods, and even ideas can be considered resources in this context.

In her 1997 examination of identity and violence in the Hebrew Bible (*The Curse of Cain: The Violent Legacy of Monotheism*, nominated for a Pulitzer Prize), Regina Schwartz broke new ground in claiming that monotheistic religions gain power and create division by way of resource scarcity. Her thesis was that "monotheism abhors, reviles, rejects, and ejects whatever it defines as outside its compass" and "forges identity antithetically" in such a way as to lead to violence against outsiders.[38] Proponents of this view (sociologist Rodney Stark, among others) believe the monotheistic image of God is most dangerous because it necessarily means that only one religion can be the true religion. Monotheistic constructs "presuppose a kind of metaphysical scarcity" in which identity formation for believers must always happen in terms of opposition to others because "limited supplies suggest boundaries."[39] Obviously, if there is only one true God and more than one tradition claims to have the correct understanding of this God, someone must be wrong. Further, since the claim that there is only one God has not resulted in a sustainable claim that there is only one true religion, internal and external conflict is inherent to monotheism.[40]

If there is only one true God then the religion of that God has a "corner on the market" of salvation. In the history of the three major monotheistic traditions we see this played out: internal conflict over the proper interpretation of the teachings of these faiths has resulted in denominational splitting and bloodshed. A few examples will suffice: in Judaism, factions fought for control of the faith and the nation during the second century BCE Maccabean Wars; in Christianity, the Protestant Reformation brought about decades of warfare as Catholics fought Protestants and Protestants fought among themselves for control; in Islam, the Shi'a Muslims trace their origins to the murder of their leader, Ali, in 661 CE by the group we know today as the Sunnis. The murder happened as a result of a struggle for power. Imam Ali, a cousin of Muhammad, and his followers believed leadership of the Muslim people should be in the hands of someone with a "blood relation" to Muhammad, whereas the Sunnis believed leadership belonged in the hands of the caliphate, or political authority, regardless of relation to Muhammad.

Since Christians insist they worship the same God as the Jews, and Muslims insist their God is the God of the Jews and Christians, one might expect that relative peace among the traditions would result. In truth the opposite has been the case. This is, according to resource-scarcity theories, because the proponents of each of these traditions have generated new scriptures and new claims about how one achieves salvation which supplant those of the parent belief systems. In the case of the monotheisms, some sacred spaces have also become contentious because of the claims of the faiths. Christianity arose out of Judaism, accepted the Jewish Bible, and added twenty-seven writings to it which are said to "complete" the Hebrew Bible. Christians believe that the God worshipped by the Jews is their God, who became incarnate in Jesus of Nazareth, and that salvation is gained through this belief. Muslims believe that Allah is the same God as that of Jews and Christians, and that the holy Quran was given by Allah to correct the errors made by human followers of the prophets who had been sent to proclaim the Truth.

Because Jesus was a first century CE Palestinian Jew, the sacred spaces of Judaism's Jerusalem are also sacred to Christians. Jesus prayed and made offerings to God at the Temple. And because Muhammad's mystical Night Journey, in which he was taken bodily into the presence of Allah in Paradise, also occurred there, Jerusalem is sacred to Muslims. This small piece of land is very much a scarce resource. There is only one Jerusalem but three monotheisms with claims to it. The Temple Mount is the site of the first and second Jewish Temples, which makes it the holiest place on earth for Jews. The Mount is also the location of two ancient holy sites for Muslims, the Dome of the Rock (from the center of which Muhammad ascended to heaven and received Allah's direction regarding prayer) and the Al Aqsa Mosque, constructed in the early eight century to mark the "farthest mosque" referred to in the Quran (Sura 17.7) where Muhammad's Night Journey ended.

Conflict over this contested sacred space has been ongoing but recently has taken on a more threatening character because of an alliance between some conservative Christians and Orthodox Jews who focus on the eagerly anticipated end times. The Jewish Temple Mount Faithful believe the Temple must be rebuilt in order for the true messiah to come. Some members believe that it is up to them to initiate the final battle that will mark the beginning of transformation of this world into the Kingdom of God, and so they have attacked Muslims in order to force the issue. In 1977, a group lead by Yehudah Etzion planted bombs in cars, attacked Palestinians, and laid plans to blow up the Dome of the Rock in order to bring about the end times.[41] The beliefs of the Temple Mount Faithful converge with that of Christian Zionists who believe the Temple must be rebuilt to bring about the second coming of Christ. The "Jerusalem Declaration on Christian Zionism," a statement issued by the Latin Patriarch and heads of local churches in Jerusalem in 2006, sums up the dangerous nature of this belief system:

> Christian Zionism is a modern theological and political movement that embraces the most extreme ideological positions of Zionism, thereby becoming detrimental to a just peace within Palestine and Israel. . . . The Gospel is identified with the ideology of empire, colonialism and militarism. . . . It places an emphasis on apocalyptic events leading to the end of history rather than living Christ's love and justice today. We categorically reject Christian Zionist doctrines as false teaching that corrupts the biblical message of love, justice and

reconciliation. We further reject the contemporary alliance of Christian Zionist leaders and organizations with elements in the governments of Israel and the United States that are presently imposing their unilateral pre-emptive borders and domination over Palestine. This inevitably leads to unending cycles of violence that undermine the security of all peoples of the Middle East and the rest of the world. We reject the teachings of Christian Zionism that facilitate and support these policies as they advance racial exclusivity and perpetual war rather than the gospel of universal love, redemption and reconciliation taught by Jesus Christ. Rather than condemn the world to the doom of Armageddon we call upon everyone to liberate themselves from the ideologies of militarism and occupation. Instead, let them pursue the healing of the nations![42]

This statement eloquently and succinctly expresses the way in which resource scarcity contributes to religious violence when religious people lay claim to sacred spaces.

## "Religioscapes"

What is an ideology without a space to which it refers, a space which it describes, whose vocabulary and kinks it makes use of, and whose code it embodies?[43]

In 1997, a year before the bombings of American embassies in Africa, Osama bin Laden gave an interview to ABC News in which he said that America deserved to be targeted by militant groups. Among the United States' list of crimes, according to bin Laden, was the occupation of "'the lands of Islam in the holiest of places, the Arabian Peninsula.'"[44] Statements like these imply that one major cause of religious violence arises out of conceptualizations of sacred space. In some forms of Islam, for example, the world is said to be divided into the realms of *Dar al-Islam*, literally "abode of submission" (to Allah) and *Dar al-Harb*, "abode of war." Although these concepts are not found in the major texts of the religion, they have functioned at times in Islamic history as a lens through which to view relations with non-Muslim people and to justify conquest of territory through violent means.

And yet, according to some analysts, it seems that the majority of terrorism, at least that done in the name of Islam since the 1990s, has been committed by Muslims for whom *Dar al-Islam* has become "deterritorialized." Many of the perpetrators of recent violent acts were Westernized Muslims, living outside of traditionally Islamic countries. They tend to be either "born-again Muslims" or converts to the faith: they "are all far more a product of a Westernized Islam than of traditional Middle Eastern politics . . . more a post-modern phenomenon than a premodern one."[45] *Dar al-Islam* once designated that part of the world where Muslims lived under Muslim rule. For these new deterritorialized Muslims, *Dar al-Islam* exists wherever Muslims live. In this new vision, Islam becomes radicalized through "expression of a reconstructed self in reference to a virtual ummah [Muslim community]."[46] Conceptualization of the world in terms of a "Muslim/Non-Muslim" religioscape implicitly and unavoidably communicates a moral geography. Moral geographies are made up of unspoken ethical assertions that influence culture and politics and denote bonds and divisions among people.[47]

It is easy to see how this worldview might contribute to justification of violence against those outside the borders of one's religio-moral mental geographic framework. The deterritorialization of these geographies opens the door to loosening of nationalist ties and the creation of global religioscapes wherein it is religious, not national, identity that matters most.

One striking instance of this phenomenon is seen in the way in which some Christian evangelical missionary denominations approach the world today. For these groups, the world is literally mapped theologically, as Christian or non-Christian (sometimes labeled "demonic"). Many of these groups participate in worldwide efforts to reach those who live in what is now called the "10/40 Window of Opportunity." This "Window" stretches from 10 to 40 degrees north of the equator, extending from North Africa through China. The region is of strategic importance to these evangelists because it contains the largest population of non-Christians on the planet and so the greatest opportunity for expansion of membership in their faith systems. The impact of this constructed religio-moral geography can be seen in the way it is played out today in Haiti, where Christian Pentecostals are waging spiritual warfare to take back the nation from Satan, with whom they believe the leader of the 1804 Haitian Revolution made a pact in exchange for freedom from colonial domination.[48]

After Vodou was officially recognized as a religion by the Haitian government in 2003 and political violence broke out with the military coup, as many as 70 percent of missionaries fled the island because they believed President Jean-Bertrand Aristide planned to renew the ancient pact with Satan on January 1, 2004,[49] but many have since returned and renewed the battle for the spiritual soul of the land and its people. Tensions are rising as escalation in the rhetoric of spiritual warfare and crusade aimed at exorcising the demonic influences from individuals and the nation occurs.

These examples clearly show the connection between monotheisms and perpetration of religious violence. However, we cannot forget that religious violence involving nonmonotheistic religions like Hinduism, Buddhism, and Jainism has occurred throughout the centuries. Religious violence seems to be a part of every form of religion. In truth, Holy War may be an "essential element of virtually all religious systems." For believers these wars are "situational moments of divine-human cooperation," a type of sacramental action performed in accordance with transcendent goals and in the service of justice, peace, and human redemption.[50] How and why this happens must be understood.


## CONCLUDING THOUGHTS: CASE STUDY OF RELIGION'S IMPACT ON VIOLENCE IN THE PHILIPPINES

Undoubtedly, the causes of religious violence are complex and intertwined. To illustrate just how much this is so, let's look briefly at the situation in Mindanao, a region in the Philippines. Conflict in the area has been ongoing for many decades and involves ethnic, religious, economic, political, and resource-scarcity issues. Today, the majority of the population on Mindanao is the Moro, who are mostly Muslim belonging to at least ten different ethnic groups. The groups have significant cultural and linguistic differences, as well as unique interpretations of Islam. Although most recent media reports have focused on terrorism and claims to ties between the Moro Islamic Liberation Front (MILF) and Al-Qaeda, a recent State Department publication indicates the causes of violence may actually be rooted less in religion than in local politics and family relations. In a 2002 privately funded survey, the Asia Foundation identified *ridu*, or clan violence, as the most common source of tension. *Ridu* is a centuries-old custom of tribal feuding. It can involve disputes among family members or between rival clans over land, money, marriage, or political power. Revenge killing is often an end result, along with expansion of the violence to include women and children of the involved tribes. *Ridu* becomes explosive when those involved use family ties to pull members of MILF and the army into the conflicts.[51]

The long history of colonial rule over the Philippines, by the Spanish from the sixteenth through nineteenth centuries and by the United States from 1899 through the end of World War II, ensured a solid foundation for Christianity over most of the islands. In the Mindanao region the situation was made more complex since Islam was fairly well established in the south by the middle of the sixteenth century, while the rest of the island groups either remained "Indios" (devotees of the indigenous animistic religion) or converted to Christianity.

Under Spanish rule, there was ongoing violence due to attempts by the Spanish government to forcibly convert the Muslim populations, whom they called "Moros," to Christianity. Later, under U.S. military rule the failure to understand that there was no centralized authority among the Moro led the governing authority to react in ways that perpetuated the instability. The U.S. governing authority established an unequal system of justice in which disputes between Moros and Christians were governed by Philippine law, but all other disputes were left to be settled by Moro custom. Private landownership was established, families were granted parcels of land, and all land sales required government approval. Inequality was made law when, in 1903, all Moro land holdings were declared null and void. In 1913, a law was passed that allowed Christians to own twice as much land as Muslims. In 1919, Christian land entitlement was extended to three times that of Muslims. These laws fed into the unrest in the region.

Once independence from the United States became imminent, the Moro leadership appealed unsuccessfully not to be included in the newly independent Philippines. The 1935 "Dansalan Declaration" stated that,

> should the US government grant the Philippines independence, the islands of Mindanao and Sulu should not be included. Our public lands must not be given to other people. . . . All our practices that are incidental to our religion Islam should be respected because these things are what a Muslim desires to live for. Once our religion is no more our lives are no more.[52]

In the 1950s, northern groups formed the New People's Army and staged a Maoist rebellion. In order to defuse the situation, the government began relocating these people to the south and giving them seized plots of Moro land. Unrest was perpetual. When martial law was finally declared in 1972, the Moros went to war; the Moro National Liberation Front (MNLF) was formed and called for an independent Moro state. Armed conflict over the next twenty-five years resulted in at least 100,000 Moro deaths and 250,000 displaced from their homes. The violence has continued to the present day.

If we reflect on this situation in light of the material we've uncovered through our search for clues to the sources of religious violence, we see that the Mindanao region is not caught up in a simple and straightforward Islamic jihad aimed at the Christian population. The region is enmeshed in violence today because of a complex interaction of multiple factors. Traditional clan customs, which may have evolved in part out of biological group selection impulses, the politics and economics of colonial rule, and resource scarcity resulting from land reallocations caused by forced or government-induced migrations appear to be the primary roots.

Were we to take a narrow view of this situation, reading it in terms of limited salvation or monotheistic resource scarcity, it would be easy to interpret this as an inevitable clash of religious ideologies. Even though Muslims and Christians ostensibly worship the same God, their claims about what this God intends for humanity diverge just enough, some might say, to escalate the particularism inherent in all monotheisms beyond the point of tolerance. Religious differences have clearly played a role in Mindanao's violent past but apparently always within the context of some other more primary driving force.

Christian exclusivist claims to salvation led in the past first to forced conversions of Muslims by Christians and then to preferential treatment of Christians by the government in granting land ownership. Resource scarcity both in terms of religious ideologies and the physical environment has played a role in perpetuating the conflict. In recent decades, some Moro groups have begun to use Islamic teachings on justice and jihad in support of the violence which began long ago and for very different reasons.

As we come to the end of this wide-ranging survey of theoretical explanations it seems clear that, whatever the form it takes, religious violence is "causally heterogeneous": cultural, economic, and political factors all play a role.[53] However, the temptation to reify these factors can be just as strong as the urge to speak of religion itself as an independent actor. Violence is committed by human beings who make choices, so without careful attention to psychology, any theory of religious violence will remain incomplete. In truth, it may well be the case that what matters most in our efforts to get to the real roots of the problem (especially in understanding suicide terrorism) is the psychology of the individual as shaped by and in interaction with the group.

Subjective interpretations of one's situation play a crucial role in the process that ends in violence. Many Americans have been surprised to learn that Al-Qaeda operatives tend to be from the more privileged sectors of their societies, to be educated and economically well-off. Their leader, Osama bin Laden, was a millionaire. So while objective conditions of injustice, lack of education, and poverty play a part in some situations, perceived injustice is more important in the long run. Individual psychology may well be the major issue, and to this issue we now turn.

## NOTES

1. Sigmund Freud, *The Future of an Illusion* (New York: W. W. Norton, 1927/1989) and *Civilization and Its Discontents* (New York: W. W. Norton, 1930/1989).

2. Jonathan Fox, *Religion, Civilization, and Civil War: 1945 through the New Millennium* (Lanham, MD: Lexington Books, 2004), 15. See also Jonathan Fox, "The Rise of Religious Nationalism and Conflict: Ethnic Conflict and Revolutionary Wars 1945–2001," *Journal of Peace Research* 41 (2004): 715–33.

3. Peter L. Berger, "The Desecularization of the World: A Global Overview," in *The Desecularization of the World: Resurgent Religion and World Politics*, ed. Peter L. Berger (Washington, DC: Ethics and Public Policy Center and Wm. B. Eerdmans, 1999), 3.

4. Richard Dawkins, *The Devil's Chaplain* (London: Weidenfield & Nicolson, 2003), 135.

5. Richard Dawkins, *The God Delusion* (New York: Bantam Books, 2006).

6. Pascal Boyer, *Religion Explained: The Evolutionary Origins of Religious Thought* (New York: Basic Books, 2001), 202, 330.

7. Scott Atran, *In Gods We Trust: The Evolutionary Landscape of Religion* (New York: Oxford University Press, 2002).

8. David Sloan Wilson, *Darwin's Cathedral: Evolution, Religion, and the Nature of Society* (Chicago: University of Chicago Press, 2002), 9, 143.

9. Ferren MacIntyre, "Was Religion a Kinship Surrogate?" *Journal of the American Academy of Religion* 72, no. 3 (2004): 653–94.

10. Holmes Ralston III, "Review of Darwin's Cathedral: Evolution, Religion, and the Nature of Society," *Journal of the American Academy of Religion* 72, no. 3 (2004): 800–803.

11. Michael Tomasello, *The Cultural Origins of Human Cognition* (Cambridge, MA: Harvard University Press, 1999), 11; Merlin Donald, *A Mind So Rare: The Evolution of Human Consciousness* (New York: W. W. Norton, 2001), xiii.

12. Center for Strategic and International Studies (CSIS), "What Is Globalization?" www.globalization101.org/What_is_Globalization.html (accessed March 3, 2007).

13. Ted Robert Gurr, "Economic Factors," in *The Roots of Terrorism*, ed. Louise Richardson (New York: Routledge, 2006), 85–86.

14. Atanas Gotchev, "Terrorism and Globalization," in *The Roots of Terrorism*, ed. Louise Richardson (New York: Routledge, 2006), 106.

15. Stanley J. Tambiah, *Leveling Crowds: Ethnonationalist Conflicts and Collective Violence in South Asia* (Berkeley: University of California Press, 1997), 5–6.

16. Quoted in Muhib O. Opeloye, "Injustice in the World Order: The Revolution of Islamic Republic of Iran as a Response," in *Imam Kohmeini and the International System: A Collection of Articles*, trans. Mansoor Limba (Tehran, Iran: Institute for Compilation and Publication of Imam Khomeini's Works, 2004),153, www.geocities .com/icpikw/intlsystem11_08.pdf (accessed March 30, 2007).

17. Quoted in Mark Jurgensmeyer, *Terror in the Mind of God: The Global Rise of Religious Violence* (Berkeley: University of California Press, 2000), 180–81.

18. Jurgensmeyer, *Terror in the Mind of God*, 10.

19. Jurgensmeyer, *Terror in the Mind of God*, 226–27.

20. Mark Jurgensmeyer, "Religion as a Cause for Terrorism," in *The Roots of Terrorism*, ed. Louise Richardson (New York: Routledge, 2006), 140.

21. Jurgensmeyer, *Terror in the Mind of God*, 195–97.

22. Rodney Stark, *One True God: Historical Consequences of Monotheism* (Princeton, NJ: Princeton University Press, 2001), 259.

23. Jurgensmeyer, *Terror in the Mind of God*, 238.

24. Ram Puniyani, "Religion: Opium of the Masses or . . ." in *Religion, Power, and Violence: Expression of Politics in Contemporary Times*, ed. Ram Puniyani (New Delhi, India: Sage, 2005), 27–43, 40–41.

25. Fox, *Religion, Civilization*, 1–2.

26. University of Maryland, Minorities at Risk Project, www.cidcm.umd.edu/inscr/ mar/(accessed February 26, 2007).

27. Political Instability Task Force, State Failure, "Internal Wars and Failures of Governance, 1955–2006," http://globalpolicy.gmu.edu/pitf/ (accessed February 26, 2007).

28. Fox, "The Rise of Religious Nationalism," 728–29.

29. Fox, *Religion, Civilization*, 233–35.

30. Jurgensmeyer, "Religion as a Cause," 141.

31. Ram Puniyani, "Introduction," in *Religion, Power, and Violence: Expression of Politics in Contemporary Times*, ed. Ram Puniyani (New Delhi, India: Sage, 2005), 12–26.

32. Stanley J. Tambiah, "Urban Riots and Cricket in South Asia: A Postscript to 'Leveling Crowds,'" *Modern Asian Studies* 39, no. 4 (2005): 897–927.

33. Tambiah, "Urban Riots," 898–99.

34. PBS, Frontline, "U.S. Military Deployment: 1969 to the Present," October 26, 2004, www.pbs.org/wgbh/pages/frontline/shows/pentagon/maps/9.html (accessed March 4, 2007).

35. Robert Pape, "Conversations with History," Institute of International Studies, UC Berkeley, http://globetrotter.berkeley.edu/people6/Pape/pape–con0.html (accessed March 2, 2007).

36. Robert Pape, *Dying to Win: The Strategic Logic of Suicide Terrorism* (New York: Random House, 2005), 20–24.

37. Elizabeth McAlister, "Globalization and the Religious Production of Space," *Journal for the Scientific Study of Religion* 44, no. 3 (2005): 249–55.

38. Regina M. Schwartz, *The Curse of Cain: The Violent Legacy of Monotheism* (Chicago: University of Chicago Press, 1997), 16.

39. Schwartz, *Curse of Cain*, 33. Identity formation will be addressed in more detail in chapter 4.

40. Stark, *One True God*, 116–17.

41. Gershon Gorenberg, *The End of Days: Fundamentalism and the Struggle for the Temple Mount* (New York: Free Press, 2000).

42. Patriarch Michel Sabbah (Latin Patriarchate, Jerusalem), Archbishop Swerios Malki Maurad (Syrian Orthodox Patriarchate, Jerusalem), Bishop Riah Abu El-Assal (Episcopal Church of Jerusalem and the Middle East), and Bishop Munib Younan (Evangelical Lutheran Church in Jordan and the Holy Land), "The Jerusalem Declaration on Christian Zionism," August 22, 2006, www.voltairenet.org/article144310 .html (accessed April 4, 2007).

43. Henri Lefebvre, *The Production of Space*, trans. Donald Nicholson Smith (Cambridge, MA: Blackwell, 1991).

44. Quoted in Jurgensmeyer, *Terror in the Mind of God*, 179.

45. Oliver Roy, "Terrorism and Deculturation," in *The Roots of Terrorism*, ed. Louise Richardson (New York: Routledge, 2006), 160–62.

46. Roy, "Terrorism and Deculturation," 162.

47. McAlister, "Globalization," 251.

48. McAlister, "Globalization," 252. Technically, Haiti isn't within the 10/40 Window, but it is a very important space for evangelicals since they see it as a territory of deeply embedded demonic influence.

49. Ken Walker, "After the Coup: Missionaries Return to Begin Rebuilding out of the Rubble," *Christianity Today* 48, no. 5 (2004): 19. See also *Christianity Today* 47, no. 10 (2003): 28.

50. Charles Selengut, *Sacred Fury: Understanding Religious Violence* (Walnut Creek, CA: AltaMira Press, 2003), 19–21.

51. "Asia Foundation Uses Media to Discuss Violence in Mindanao; Partnership for a Better Life," 2007 Federal Information and News Dispatch, Inc., State Department Documents and Publications, February 12, 2007, LexisNexis.

52. Salah Jubair, *Bangsamoro—A Nation Under Endless Tyranny* (Lahore, Pakistan: Islamic Research Academy, 1984), 46–48.

53. Tambiah, "Urban Riots," 920.

*Chapter Four*

# What Psychology Has to Offer

The 1999 U.S. government's profile of terrorists notes that although the social psychology of terrorism has received extensive analysis, "the individual
psychology of political and religious terrorism has been largely ignored."[1]
Perhaps one reason for this may be that scholars have until recently shared the
opinion, expressed by prominent sociologist Rodney Stark, that psychology
can only be a "cul-de-sac" because violence varies cross-culturally and historically: "The causes of phenomena such as religious conflict are not to be
found primarily within the human head, unless we make the patently false assumption that basic psychological processes differ greatly by time and
place."[2] As we shall see, though, particularly in terms of terrorist activity, the
psychological is in fact primary. What matters most is precisely what goes on
in the human head; the subjective experience of injustice or deprivation matters far more than the conditions of objective reality. People climb up the
"staircase to terrorism" because of how they perceive their situations, which
are often objectively those of middle-class citizens who have the agency and
resources necessary to shape their own futures.[3] In this chapter we will examine some of the major psychological explanations offered for violent religious behaviors and will discover that the material uncovered leads us not
into a cul-de-sac but rather down new and potentially fruitful paths toward
elimination of the causes.

While there is no shortage of work published on the psychology of religious violence, very little has yet been done in terms of psychodynamics.[4]
This is unfortunate since psychoanalytic and depth psychology theories provide very powerful resources for uncovering the factors that influence individual motivation and behavior, and may well provide the most comprehensive framework for understanding religion that we have today.[5] As noted

previously, the authors of the U.S. government's terrorist profile document point out that the majority of attention to religious violence from the standpoint of psychology has up until now come from social psychology. We will therefore start our exploration with this research but always with the goal of uncovering the dynamics of religious violence operating at the level of the individual believer. If we are to make progress toward the goal of empowering individuals to take some measure of responsibility for long-term amelioration of this age-old problem, we must understand the problem from the perspective of the individual actor.

## SOCIAL PSYCHOLOGY AND RELIGIOUS VIOLENCE

Before exploring themes in social psychological research, it is important to note that there is no consensus among psychologists and psychiatrists on the causes of terrorism in any form, and the addition of religion to the mix complicates understanding even further. Social psychologists study how the individual's beliefs and behaviors are shaped by the social group. Theories are usually developed using experimental methods like questionnaire analysis or manipulation of situations in controlled settings, with the aim of gathering data to be used in developing theories that are applicable to humanity as a whole.

From a social psychology view, religion is perhaps most understandable in terms of meaning system analysis. In psychology, a meaning system is a set of particular beliefs and theories about ourselves, others, and the world that functions as the lens through which we view reality. Religious meaning systems are distinctive because they are comprehensive, central to global understandings, and focused on what is considered sacred. Because they operate at both the individual and collective levels, consciously or subconsciously, religious meaning systems tend to be seen as sources of fundamental incontrovertible truths. As such, religious ideas can facilitate violence in a number of ways.

Religious teachings frequently disseminate ideas that aid the development of a sense of privilege or election among believers which can serve as an inducement to intolerance of those not perceived to be among the elect. This trend toward bias can also be encouraged by absolutist teachings that claim there is only one path to salvation. One example, as we have seen, is teachings on selflessness and self-sacrifice; these principles have at times been interpreted so as to encourage participation in warfare. In some religious systems leaders have perverted teachings on selflessness to mean willingness to die in conflict conducted on behalf of the system's transcendent goals.

Because religious teachings function as moral frameworks it is possible to legitimize violence through sanctification of such action. Once an act has been sanctified, or made holy, by its association with the will of the divine, the believer may engage in violence with impunity even if it contradicts general moral teachings of the faith. Through a process of moral disengagement and cognitive redefinition, it becomes acceptable, for example, for a Christian to kill another person in order to eliminate evil in the world. Among the cognitive tools deployed in service of moral disengagement are the use of euphemisms and dehumanizing rhetoric which demonizes those outside the religious community. When violence is described as a means for achieving peace or spreading God's Word it is no longer violence but has become holy action done on behalf of God. When our enemies are not conceived of as fellow humans but as infidels, gooks, agents of the Antichrist, vermin, Christ-killers, spawn of the Devil, and so forth, it becomes much easier to justify their elimination.[6] Additionally, the powerful meaning systems of religious ideas can work to support violence because they can provide a ready-made organizational complex which enhances dissemination of information, mechanisms for personalizing the conflict (since one's own eternal well-being is at stake), imagery of cosmic conflict that supports absolutizing rhetoric, and ultimate transhistorical meaning.[7]

Religions, then, as meaning systems provide a ready scaffolding that can support violence; but very often, religious issues come into play only after other ground floor conditions have prepared the way for escalation of tensions. Religion can sometimes become the vehicle of expression for issues that were not initially religious in nature. It is important to keep in mind that religion alone, even though often powerfully influential in the evolution of violence, is not sufficient as an explanation for it. In a masterful study on the psychology of genocide and mass murder, James Waller makes a compelling case for the claim that ideological commitment, whether religious or otherwise, does not in and of itself explain the willingness with which human beings kill one another.[8]

## The Road to Mass Killing and Genocide

How do ordinary law-abiding citizens become willing participants in acts of brutality against other human beings? In his attempt to answer this question, James Waller has synthesized volumes of information in what may well be the most far-reaching social psychological examination of what he calls human evil (defined behaviorally as "the deliberate harming of humans by other humans"[9]).

The first factor to consider here is the impact of group dynamics. As a social psychologist, Waller is naturally concerned to understand how the group

affects the individual and notes that group interaction can function as an am-
plifier that intensifies the tendencies within the group. Isolated groups tend to
become more extreme in rhetoric and actions than the individuals apart from
the group would otherwise. Waller rightly insists, though, that the dynamics
of any group can only be understood in terms of the wills of the individual
group members. A group is, in other words, perhaps more a reflection of the
character of its membership than the shaper of individual actions. When we
imbue a group with powers distinct from the nature of the people who make
up the group, we are guilty of reification that allows misplaced blaming.
Group membership does not transform us into murderers unless the individual tendencies of members are predisposed in this direction. This is born out
by the fact that groups made up of individuals with positive aims tend to accomplish more good together than would be possible separately.[10] When religious individuals who believe that violence against humanity is consonant
with transcendent goals (the "will of God") gather together, group readiness
to commit violence becomes much greater than any one individual's motivation alone.

Waller reminds us that by far the majority of people who participated in the
genocides and mass killings of the twentieth century were not psychopathic—
they were ordinary people. This is clearly so, as only a very small portion of
the population suffers from psychopathy but many hundreds of thousands of
people participated in the genocides and mass murders of the twentieth century: thousands of Turks participated in the elimination of two million Ar-
menian Christians from 1915 to 1923; hundreds of thousands of Germans facilitated the extermination of seventeen million Jews, Gypsies, people judged
mentally incompetent or cognitively disabled, homosexuals, and other unde-
sirables during the Nazi regime; and hundreds of thousands of Hutus worked
in Rwanda to slaughter eight hundred thousand Tutus in just one hundred
days during 1994. In the case of the Nazi genocide, we have records of psy-
chiatric evaluations of Nazi war criminals and interviews with survivors of
death camps. These documents overwhelming demonstrate that no more than
5 to 10 percent of the active participants in the slaughter suffered from mental illness. In fact, the so-called sociopath or psychopath (antisocial personality disorder or APD) is far less likely to participate in genocide than normal
men and women because the sociopath has difficulty functioning as a coop-
erative member of groups. Based on the incidence of APD in the general population of men in the United States, which is about 3 percent, 97 out of every
100 actors in genocide are likely clinically normal.[11] What happens to turn
normal neighbors into murderers, whatever the ideological commitments?
What is it about human beings that makes it possible for average, psychologically healthy men and women to commit atrocities?

Waller's explanatory model posits that we become participants in such acts of evil as a result of numerous ultimate and proximal influences. An ultimate cause is the earliest factor or deepest influence that accounts for human violence, and the proximal causes are the immediate factors that operate in "real time." The ultimate causes of human violence originate in our common evolutionary history, whereas the proximate influences originate in cultural, psychological, and social constructions.

Psychologists have been making use of theories of biological evolution to come to a deeper understanding of the human mind since the 1960s. Waller's interpretation of this relatively new field of evolutionary psychology (EP) helps us to better understand the ubiquity of violence in human history. According to this mode of thought, human behavior is pushed by "universal reasoning circuits" that evolved through natural selection. The process of natural selection is one by which adaptive traits (those which enhance reproductive fitness) that can be inherited are passed on while maladaptive traits tend to fade away over succeeding generations. On this basis, EP theorists argue that behaviors present among human beings today originally evolved to solve problems of adaptation in the distant past, and at the deepest level, there is a kind of innate psychological unity among human beings. The ultimate cause of violence, then, is the "universal, evolved psychological architecture" containing elements that "leave us evolutionarily primed with the capacity for evil [violence]." Prosocial behaviors like altruism augment within-group cooperation; more negative behaviors like aggression and competition lead to "between group nastiness."[12] In Waller's formulation, religious violence, as one form of between-group nastiness, may once have been adaptive; it is perhaps an expression of tendencies and instinctual behaviors that originally evolved to enhance survival. Such violence could be seen as an atavistic trait—a "throwback" to primitive, once useful behaviors that are no longer advantageous to the survival of humanity. As Waller puts it, the ultimate influence of evolution answers "why" we are violent, whereas the "how" is answered by proximate causes.

Proximate influences include the cultural construction of worldviews, the psychological construction of "otherness," and the social construction of cruelty. These three are active influences, working together in this world to shape our behavior today. When these more immediate influences converge they activate the fundamental evolved capacity for between-group malevolence with the end result all too frequently being warfare.

Waller's discussion of cultural construction and worldviews resonates with our discussion of worldviews and religious beliefs. Our values, ideas of right and wrong, how we understand ourselves in relation to authority and social position, are all shaped by the cultures in which we live. In terms of values, cultures can be classified broadly as one of two types according to the focus on either individualistic or collectivistic good. Individualistic cultures value personal independence, achievement, and happiness. Groups do matter in individualistic cultures but only insofar as they promote the good of the individual. Groups come and go in response to the needs of individuals. The actual membership in long-standing groups tends to fluctuate and so nonmember others may be seen as less threatening than happens in collectivistic cultures.

The collectivistic culture is centered on issues related to belonging: conformity, tradition, obedience, and order. One's personal identity is defined in terms of group membership, which tends to be fixed and stable since it is often a reflection of shared histories. Conflict in collectivistic cultures tends, then, to be between groups. Here, social identity is more important than individual identity. Waller says that in-group/out-group distinctions are more likely to arise and end in conflict in collectivistic cultures. He gives the example of genocidal regimes like the Hutu of Rwanda, who define human identity in terms of "Hutuness," and the Nazis, who defined "humanness" in terms of Aryan bloodlines. Cultural worldviews that order reality in terms of authority and position in social hierarchies are especially prone to convergence with evolutionary tendencies so as to result in behaviors that harm others.[13]

Humans have evolved a very powerful protective psychological mechanism that comes into play when we are faced with the choice to participate in violence. Waller calls it the "psychological construction of the 'other.'" Basically, the less like "us" someone or something is perceived to be, the easier it is to kill it. At its most basic level construction of "otherness" is an outgrowth of grouping behavior. When groups form among humans, even if there is no genetic relationship or other similarity among members, we very quickly and easily develop a sense of the boundary separating "us" from "them" and a bias toward the in-group through a kind of pseudo-kinship. Our propensity to in-group affiliation is illustrated by social psychological research. In the Robber's Cave Experiment, twenty-two normal eleven-year-old boys camped together for three weeks as part of a study on group behavior. The boys were randomly assigned to one of two cabins situated some distance apart. The researchers set up competitive activities, games, and other situations designed to pit one group against the other. Within a week, each group had named itself (Rattlers and Eagles), chosen a leader, and begun to develop a distinctive group culture. Conflict erupted quickly, and the tension became so high that even watching a movie would quickly devolve into fighting between the two groups.[14]

As a group enters into us-them thinking and engages in aggression toward the other, human psychological defenses expand to distance "us" further from "them." These defenses include moral disengagement, through which we justify our actions and dehumanize the other, and blaming the victims of our aggression. Moral disengagement is an active (and largely unconscious) uncoupling process by which others are gradually moved outside the arena within which moral values operate. This process is enhanced in situations where reification of groups and ideologies is in operation.

Disengagement is augmented by language that dehumanizes the other. Use of slang terms for outsiders is one very common example. This happens at all levels of social organization, from normal teenagers in America with their complex taxonomy of otherness (including labels like hoods, geeks, nerds, jocks, preppies, Goths, stoners, and so on) to the more formalized process of government-sponsored propaganda aimed at representing the enemy in less-than-human terms (like American World War II depictions of Japanese soldiers as apes in military garb, or medieval Christian European depictions of Jewish people as horned minions of the devil).

Another technique that aids in psychological and moral disengagement is the use of euphemisms for actions which in normal morality are considered atrocities. "Number of civilian dead" becomes "collateral damage" for American military bombing targets in the Iraq war; mass murder becomes "the Final Solution" for Nazi Germany and "ethnic cleansing" for Bosnia. When added to the belief (implicit in dehumanizing rhetoric) that the targets of such activity deserve to be eliminated, we have the ingredients for development of the "just world phenomenon." This is an intriguing mental maneuver that often "kicks in" when our conviction that the world is a just place is threatened. In the case of genocide, for example, the victims must be conceptualized so as to allow the perpetrators to see their actions as one manifestation of justice—thus, blaming the victim is crucial. If we can convince ourselves that the Other deserves extermination we can live more comfortably with our atrocities. The connection to religion is especially obvious here. The monotheistic worldviews place great importance of conceptualization of God as just, so if a believer can portray her actions to eliminate the "spawn of Satan" as done in the service of divine justice, all the better.

The final piece of Waller's answer to the puzzling question of how nice, normal, law-abiding citizens can be transformed into amoral killers is the mechanism of social constructions of cruelty. When the cultural construction of worldviews conducive to violence and psychological construction of other-as-threat arise in the right (wrong?) circumstances, all the ingredients are in place for an atrocity-producing situation. Research shows that personality variables only explain a very small percentage of variance in human behavior: "Individual behavior is largely under the control of social forces and environmental contingencies rather than personality traits, character, will power."[15] Two seminal research projects (along with a large number of subsequent studies) underscore how powerful social context is for our conceptions of cruelty: Stanley Milgram's research on obedience and Philip Zimbardo's Stanford Prison Experiment. These studies show how easily average mentally healthy men and women can be induced to perpetrate acts of cruelty for little or no reason, and will help shed light on the individual's responsibility for group violence.

In Milgram's experiment, subjects were told that the study would investigate the impact of punishment on learning. Each subject was led to believe that positions of "teacher" or "learner" had been assigned randomly, but in truth the "teacher" position always fell to the actual subject whose responses were under examination, and the "learner" was always one of the experimental team. All instructions were given by an experimenter dressed in a white lab coat. The "learner" was taken into a small room, strapped into a chair, and had an electrode that was connected to a "generator" taped to his arm (in the original experiment, all participants were men). The "teacher," who was able to hear the learner via an intercom, sat in front of a panel of switches that were said to control the shock generator. The panel had thirty switches labeled as generating voltage in 15 volt increments ranging from 15 to 450. Switch labels also included verbal indicators of severity like "Slight Shock" and "Danger: Severe Shock," and the two highest levels were labeled XXX. The teacher's task was to read a list of words to the learner and administer shocks whenever the learner made a mistake.

Unbeknownst to the true subjects of the experiment, the learner received no actual shock at all. He deliberately made mistakes, and when the teacher increased the punishment voltage he acted as though he was experiencing intense pain. The learner even went so far as to complain that he had a bad heart condition, exclaimed "I can't take it any more!" "You have no right to keep me here!" Once the shocks reached 330 volts and beyond, the learner stopped responding altogether. The experimenter in the lab coat calmly encouraged the "teacher" to continue, offering reassurance that he, not the teacher, would take full responsibility for the outcome.[16]

A panel of forty psychiatrists was asked to predict how many subjects would continue with the experiment to the point of administering upper ranges of voltage. They predicted that the majority would drop out at 150 volts, and less than 1 percent would be willing to go all the way to the end. In actuality, 65 percent of subjects went all the way to 450 volts. Later replication experiments done between 1963 and 1985 found a compliance rate ranging from 31 to 91 percent in the United States and, in other nations, from 28 (Australia) to 88 percent (South Africa).[17]

In August of 1971, Stanford social psychologist Philip Zimbardo set up an experiment designed to test the conditions under which violence arises in prisons. Zimbardo's research team set up a very realistic prison setting in the basement of the campus psychology building and arranged to have ten of twenty-one young male volunteers "arrested" at their homes by local off-duty police for what was to be a fourteen-day around-the-clock experiment aimed at studying prisoner psychology. The participants had been screened to ensure they were mentally and physically healthy, and randomly assigned to play either prison guard or prisoner. The guards wore uniforms, carried police-type night sticks, and were told their job was to maintain order and observe the prisoners. They were to create as realistic an environment as possible without use of physical punishment. The prisoners were stripped, were sprayed with a powder (to mimic the delousing then administered at real prisons), were issued numbered uniforms, and had a nylon stocking put on their heads to simulate head-shaving. The cells were monitored by audio but not video surveillance.

The apparent ease and rapidity with which participants fell into their assigned roles is disturbing. It became apparent within the first few days that some of the young men lost conscious awareness that the situation was not real, and that all seemed to have done so before the experiment ended. Three prisoners had to be released from the experiment in the first four days because of intense negative psychological reactions ranging from confused thinking to hysterical crying. A fourth had to be released when he developed a severe rash after the mock parole board denied his petition for release. As for the guards, Zimbardo reports that it was frightening to see how easily and quickly these young men fell into a pattern of escalating degrading and sadistic behavior. Sexual harassment by guards began to develop on the fourth day and fully blossomed on the nightshift of the fifth, leading to an abrupt and early end to the whole enterprise. On that night, three prisoners who had failed to comply adequately with some order from a guard were singled out to be humiliated. Dressed in hospital-type gowns and no underwear, the three young men were ordered to bend over and touch their toes. Two other prisoners were ordered to stand behind the "female camels" and "hump them," while the guards aggressively heaped on verbal abuse. The transformation of these normal young men into sadistic tormentors was so disturbing that when Zimbardo learned of the incident the next morning, he had to shut down the experiment. All of this transpired before even one week was out.[18] Writing about all of this recently, Zimbardo said,

[The participants] all began the experience as seemingly good people. Those who were guards knew that but for the random flip of a coin they could have been wearing the prisoner smocks and been controlled by those they were now abusing. They also knew that the prisoners had done nothing criminally wrong. . . . Yet, some guards have transformed into perpetrators of evil, and other guards have become passive contributors to the evil through their inaction. Still other normal, healthy young men as prisoners have broken down under the situational pressures, while the remaining surviving prisoners have become zombie-like followers.[19]

The outcome of the experiment was so shockingly painful that, says Zimbardo, he was unable to complete a book on the project until thirty years later. It was only after he was asked to serve as an expert witness for one of the American military guards charged with gross prisoner abuse in 2004 at Abu Ghraib Prison in Iraq that he was able to return to the earlier work and write a complete account. The parallels between Abu Ghraib and the Stanford experiment are stunning. Zimbardo's analysis shows how susceptible to social context human morality and behavior can be.

Western cultural understandings run counter to these research findings which tell us that situational factors are, under the right conditions, more powerful than basic personality tendencies. In American culture, for example, the dispositional rather than situational view is dominant, and so we find it hard to accept these discoveries. Western medicine, psychiatry, law, and religion operate on the assumption that when wrongs are committed, culpability lies with the individual. Situations like those explored in the Milgram and Zimbardo experiments show us this is, more often than not, counter to the way things really are. All the more shocked then are we to learn how easily that, given the right conditions, normal morality can be turned completely on its head.

Under certain conditions, what is wrong becomes right, killing becomes a means of healing, and atrocity becomes acceptable. If, as the Milgram and Zimbardo experiments indicate, ordinary members of this American individualistic culture are so easily affected by the situation in which they find themselves, becoming subject to authority and so easily induced, simply by virtue of situational factors and role expectations, to commit abuses like these, how much more powerful this must be in authoritarian and collectivistic cultures!

Although Waller's distinctions between individualistic and collectivistic cultures seem clear, we must not lose sight of the fact that individualistic values are shaped by the collective. Social Identity Theory tells us the main factor that determines sources of identity is group power. Authentic individual identity can only be developed in the context of group identity: "Individual authenticity arises from collective authenticity; more broadly, individual consciousness arises from collective consciousness."[20] Even American "rugged individualism" is shaped in this way—it has no meaning outside the shared ethos of American values.

## Theoretical Application to Religious Violence

It will be helpful to pause briefly in our examination of psychology's contribution to our project and apply the discoveries made thus far to religious violence. The interaction of religious belief, as one of the most powerful constructions of meaning for human beings, with the factors that explain how we come to participate in evil acts is fascinating. Studies show that religious people tend to be more accepting of authority, perhaps making them more likely to fall into unquestioning obedience. Those traditions that have a strictly hierarchical framework would be especially so. This could, for example, help to explain the willing participation of Roman Catholic nuns and priests in the Nazi program of euthanizing at least one hundred thousand cognitively disabled and mentally ill patients in hospitals during World War II. The Roman Catholic faith emphasizes God's authority as embodied by the pope, who is called the Holy Father and speaks as God's representative to the faithful. This investment of divine authority in a human being sets the stage for unquestioning obedience to other forms of authoritarianism.

In addition to the positive correlation between religiousness and authoritarianism, studies have consistently shown religiosity to be correlated with ethnocentrism, intolerance of ambiguity, rigidity, and (among American conservative Protestants especially) racial prejudice.[21] Religious expression historically has tended to be especially prone to development of boundaries of separation between believers and nonbelievers, which clearly encourages constructions of "otherness" and us-versus-them thinking.

In terms of dehumanization and "blaming the victim," many examples could be cited. Christians have dehumanized the Jews, called them Satan's minions, and used this as sufficient reason for pogroms. In Islamic history, slaughter of nonbelievers has been supported by labeling outsiders as infidels deserving of death if they refuse to worship Allah. Religious beliefs function to shape understandings of cruelty through such practices as preaching crusade or jihad, and in this way, atrocity becomes the work (obviously morally justified) of God.

## Social Identity and Personal Humiliation

As we have learned, from the religious terrorist's point of view, violence is a rational problem-solving strategy—the world needs to be reformed, governments are failing to provide what people need in life, and so it is up to believers themselves to bring about transformation. Central among underlying factors driving radical Islamic jihadists, for example, may be a crisis of identity in Islamic cultures. The process of globalization is "steamrolling" over cultural differences and has made identity formation complicated for many groups. The West, as the main source of movies, television programs, and magazines, has come to function as the most powerful group and in the process become definitive of identity in the so-called modern world. Attempts to end violence are not yet working because they are reactionary, targeting people whose identities have already been shaped so that for them it has be-come reasonable to accept bloodshed as an option.[22]

Mark Jurgensmeyer, in his widely read *Terror in the Mind of God*, posits that "guys throw bombs" as a reaction to humiliation and emasculation re-sulting from economic frustrations. Religious ideas do add a potent "sym-bolic empowerment" dimension to the violence through which "guys" are able to assert masculinity threatened by the consequences of secularization and modernization. "Nothing is more intimate than sexuality, and no greater humiliation can be experienced than failure over what one perceives to be one's sexual role," says Jurgensmeyer.[23]

As I read it, Jurgensmeyer interprets religious violence primarily in terms of the psychological world of young men living in areas that have suffered ongoing economic and political upheaval. In a chapter entitled "Warrior's Power," he declares that the chief explanation for religious violence is that young men throw bombs "as an assertion of masculinity and a recovery of public virility that is at once sexual, social, and political."[24] Further, he says religious violence is often a device "for symbolic empowerment in wars that cannot be won and for goals that cannot be achieved," which he believes ex-plains the apocalyptic tone of much terrorist rhetoric.[25] For Jurgensmeyer, na-tional and individual humiliations are central causes of religious violence. He addresses economic and social issues *as they contribute* to the sense of emas-culation and frustration of young men.

While this analysis is accurate in some cases, it does not work well as an explanatory framework across the board. As one example, when applied to the hijackers responsible for the attacks in the United States on September 11, 2001, we see this theory fall short. The perpetrators of the 9/11 attacks were not emasculated and disenfranchised men suffering from uncertain futures. All came from what we might consider good backgrounds; they were from well-off or middle-class and moderately religious families. Most were Saudi Arabians who were not exceptional in any way prior to the events of 9/11. Many of them had attended university in Riyadh or Jeddah, Saudi Arabia. Three had been students of Islamic law. Mohamad Atta, the pilot of the first airplane, had done graduate work in architecture and urban planning at Ger-man universities. Several were married. The common thread connecting these young men was a radical interpretation of Islam that holds violent jihad as the ideal form of action.[26] Radical Islam and jihad had become obsessions for these young, intelligent men:

> Studies were abandoned, families ignored, the outer world denied as they plunged themselves into their fanatical version of faith. As a German investigator put it: "They are not talking about daily life stuff, such as buying cars—they buy cars, but they don't talk about it, they talk about religion most of the time . . . these peo-

ple are just living for their religion, meaning for them that they just live now for their life after death, the paradise. They want to live obeying their God, so they can enter paradise. Everything else doesn't matter." Talking one week of Kosovo, the next of Chechnya or Afghanistan, the "men were agreed: they wanted to fight—they just didn't know which war."[27]

Clark McCauley, a social psychologist at Bryn Mawr College, analyzed the written material found in the luggage of the 9/11 terrorists and concluded that these men acted not to right human wrongs, nor out of anger or frustration, but "with God and for God against evil . . . it is a psychology of attachment to the good rather than a psychology of hatred for evil."[28]

This discussion of the participants in the 9/11 violence helps us to see the dangers of reductionism inherent in some psychological analyses, but that is not to say that there is nothing of value in this work. Albeit something of an overgeneralization, Jurgensmeyer's thesis does add to the conversation an important element: humiliation is likely a significant psychological factor for those who commit violence in the name of their gods. Nevertheless, we must be clear; it is not simply humiliation in terms of challenges to sexual identity or emasculation due to socioeconomic disenfranchisement. While it is certainly the case that convergence of sociological conditions like collectivistic cultural milieus and demoralizing socioeconomic circumstances are often fertile soil for religious violence, these are not sufficient explanatory factors for understanding the importance of humiliation. It is rather that humiliation operates in relation to individual religious ideologies and the psychodynamic process of idealization. The secularization process often has the effect of destabilizing the God-image within collectivistic cultures, and as we shall see, it is this process that may well be both necessarily and sufficiently causative. It is the impact of this destabilization within the psyche of individuals that we need to understand, and here psychoanalysis, with its focus on the individual psyche, can be most helpful.

## MOVING TOWARD PSYCHOANALYSIS

Psychoanalytic examination of religions has come a long way since Sigmund Freud's explanation of religious ideas as nothing more than wish fulfillment and of God as a psychological projection of unresolved oedipal issues. Theories of this type differ from those discussed thus far in that they are grounded in clinical experience rather than on survey analysis or laboratory experiment. There are numerous schools of thought in psychoanalysis today, two of which will be explored in depth in the next chapter, and a hybrid approach called Terror Management Theory (TMT), which will be examined in depth here as a transition from the laboratory to the clinician's office. TMT has been developed by psychologists who want to bridge the gap between clinical psychoanalysis and the laboratory with theoretical constructs that are grounded in evolutionary theory and, as such, will help us develop connections between these first chapters and the constructive portion of this work.

TMT is a very robust conceptual system that proponents say rests on a substantial body of empirical confirmation. TMT is the creation of a group of social psychologists who were deeply influenced by anthropologist/psychiatrist Ernst Becker's work on denial of the reality of death as the source of all human motivations. Starting from the premise that facing the fact of our mortality has the potential to create in us overwhelming terror, TMT theorists speculate that uniquely human motivations arise from the tension between our biological instinct for self-preservation and our awareness of the reality of death. In evolutionary terms, this existential anxiety is not adaptive but rather a regrettable by-product of survival adaptations.[29]

Human cultural groups manage the ever-present nascent terror by constructing worldviews that resolve our existential panic in the face of death. Cultures instill in individuals a sense of themselves as valuable in a world that has meaning; this is called "self-esteem" in TMT. In this theory, self-esteem is considered vital, so it is thought that we expend a great deal of human energy in activities that help us maintain faith in our worldviews. Since our personal sense of self-worth is tied to the cultural worldview, it is important to believe that one's worldview is correct. If we live up to the expectations and values of our cultures we "will experience positive outcomes and ultimately qualify for death transcendence."[30]

In light of the fact that this is a symbolic rather than concrete solution to the problem of mortality, no cultural framework can ever totally erase the terror provoked by death awareness. We live, therefore, with a residual repressed anxiety that must be dealt with in some way. Humans most commonly cope by projection of the anxiety outward onto scapegoats identified by the group as the cause and so are considered to be in some sense evil.

Since our worldviews are at the deepest level about the denial of death, encounters with others who hold different beliefs create psychological turmoil. Should we entertain the possibility that another group's beliefs might have validity, we run the risk of letting loose the terror normally diminished by the faith we invest in our worldviews. According to TMT, none of this results in conscious awareness in the form of emotional responses. In fact, say TMT experts, the fears aroused by awareness of death exert influence most noticeably when the perception of mortality happens on the fringes of consciousness.

The mechanics of the terror management process, then, involve the activation of a set of proximal and distal psychological defenses: awareness of death stimulates suppression and rationalization through techniques like distraction and minimizing (proximal defenses) that decrease consciousness of death but increase unconscious awareness. The unconscious awareness activates the distal mechanisms of worldview defense (through increased pride in nation, group, gender, etc.) and efforts to shore up self-esteem, a process that reduces death thoughts and defuses the potential terror.[31]

There is a substantial body of research in support of the basic theory. Studies show that consideration of the inevitability of one's own death affects actual behavior specifically by provoking physical distancing from, negative attitudes toward, and physical aggression against people who hold different worldviews. The connection with self-image (defined as "feeling good about oneself") has been demonstrated in studies, as well: when people receive positive personal feedback and then are exposed to criticism of or challenges to their worldviews, they are less likely to react negatively to these challenges than subjects who received neutral or negative information.

Humans exhibit a variety of reactions to different others, all of which, according to TMT, are motivated by the need to hold the terror of death at bay. These reactions range from conversion to combat. When faced with conflicting worldviews, our least likely response is conversion to the alternative conception of reality. This has some empirical support: research shows that just before converting to a new religious or political group, people display high fear of death and low self-esteem, which reverse immediately after conversion.[32] Much more likely responses are demeaning the other, assimilation of others into one's own worldview, or accommodation. Should these methods fail to defuse the threat, the most extreme and at the same time effective approach is to eliminate the problem through annihilation of the other.

## Theoretical Application to Religious Violence

Applying Terror Management Theory to historical events, we can see these mechanisms at work. An excellent example is the way medieval European Christians dealt with Judaism. The mainstream theological position regarding other religions then was that Christianity contained the absolute truth which meant that it was the only valid religion. Jesus was the long-awaited Jewish messiah, so many of the practices and beliefs of the Jews were thought to have been superseded by the teachings of Jesus and Paul. The ongoing vitality of Judaism and even the very presence of Jews, who loved, lived, and even prospered as they worshipped the God of the "Old Testament," was therefore an affront. Jews, who by definition did not accept that the messiah had come, were a constant challenge to the Christian worldview.

Persecution of Jews had happened from time to time prior to the first crusade in 1095 CE, but persecutions increased dramatically from then on. Terror Management Theory offers an explanation for why, once Europeans became aware of Islam, which posed yet another challenge to the Christian claims to Absolute Truth, violence intensified. The threat to the Christian worldview came now from two directions. It had to be contained somehow, and violence was the end result.

Although TMT is a theory developed to explore the general social context of death terror rather than for the profiling of individuals, we can more clearly see how the proximal and distal defense mechanisms work in the case of medieval Christian treatment of the Jews by applying it to a particular theologian's work. Martin Luther (1483–1546), as one of the most influential figures in Western European and Christian history, serves as a kind of archetype of medieval Christian ideology.

Early in his reform efforts Luther attempted to deal with the challenge that Judaism presented to his worldview by encouraging fellow Christians to stop demeaning and persecuting the Jews and work to assimilate them. In 1523, he wrote a pamphlet on Jewish-Christian relations entitled "Jesus Christ Was a Jew by Birth." In it he expressed concern that Jews would never convert to Christianity if Christians continued to treat them poorly. He was certain that they had only refused conversion for so long because of the corruption of the Roman Church. Once they learned of the reform movement, Luther was convinced they would come to see the "light." He said,

> I would request and advise that one deal gently with [the Jews] and instruct them from Scripture; then some of them may come along. Instead of this we are trying only to drive them by force, slandering them, . . . when we forbid them to labor and do business and have any human fellowship with us, thereby forcing them into usury, how is that supposed to do them any good? . . . We must receive them cordially, and permit them to trade and work with us, that they may have occasion and opportunity to associate with us, hear our Christian teaching, and witness our Christian life. If some of them should prove stiff-necked, what of it? After all, we ourselves are not all good Christians either.[33]

Needless to say, Jews did not convert in droves as a result of Luther's and other reformers efforts to eliminate corruption in the church hierarchy, and Luther's early conciliatory attitude vanished by the end of his life. In 1543, three years before his death, he authored a brutal and abusive tirade against the Jews that looks to modern-day readers like a blueprint for the twentieth-century Nazi program of elimination. Luther advised leaders as follows:

> First, to set fire to [the Jews'] synagogues or schools. . . . Second, I advise that their houses also be razed and destroyed. . . . Third, I advise that all their prayer books and Talmudic writings, in which such idolatry, lies, cursing, and blasphemy are taught, be taken from them. . . . Fourth, I advise that their rabbis be forbidden to teach henceforth on pain of loss of life and limb. . . . Fifth, I advise

that safe-conduct on the highways be abolished completely for the Jews. . . .
Sixth, I advise that usury be prohibited to them, and that all cash and treasure of
silver and gold be taken from them and put aside for safekeeping. . . . Seventh,
I recommend putting a flail, an ax, a hoe, a spade, a distaff, or a spindle into the
hands of young, strong Jews and Jewesses and letting them earn their bread in
the sweat of their brow.[34]

How might we account for this drastic about-face? Viewed through the lens
of Terror Management Theory, it makes sense.

First, in spite of Luther's conviction that the only thing standing between
the Jews and conversion to Christianity was the corruption of the church leadership, his revisions of theology and practice did not result in their wholesale
conversion. The continued refusal of the Jews to accept that Christianity was
the absolute truth now constituted a double challenge: if even Luther's kinder,
gentler Christianity did not win them over, questions about worldview validity would have been intensified for him at the level of the unconscious.

By the end of his life, Luther's reform efforts had unleashed such a tremendous amount of energy amongst European Christians that challenges to his
worldview proliferated. No longer did he have only the Roman Church hierarchy and the Jews with which to contend; he was excommunicated and also
found himself battling against fellow reformers on interpretation of doctrine.
The reform movement almost immediately began to splinter, and to make
matters much worse, by 1543 the Muslim challenge had become a real threat
to Europe again. Constantinople had fallen to Islamic forces in 1453, and during Luther's life, the Ottoman Turks under the rule of Suleiman the Magnificent (1520–1566) took control of (present-day) Serbia and Montenegro and
Hungary, and besieged but failed to conquer Vienna, Austria.

At the individual level, then, Luther's own need for defense against terror
would have been greatly intensified by the 1540s. Terror Management Theory allows us to see the polemic against the Jews as a product of activated distal mechanisms of worldview defense and efforts to shore up self-esteem by
demeaning and advocating total control over the Jews, which would theoret-
ically have reduced death thoughts and defused his deep-seated terror.

## How Useful Is TMT?

Although TMT appears to be quite useful in a post-hoc analysis of our tendency to commit violent acts against others, it has not gone without critique.
First, the central claim that *all* human behavior is motivated by desire for self-
preservation and fear of death is considered problematic by many psychologists. The simple fact that people commit suicide erodes the foundation on
which TMT rests; choosing death by one's own hand shows there must be

other motivations at work in human experience. Additionally, in all the studies done to test TMT, none of the subjects reported or displayed actual signs of terror. In the substantial body of research literature on causes of anxiety, it appears that fear of social exclusion is more motivational than fear of death.[35]

Another criticism is that perhaps TMT is so useful as an after-the-fact analysis because it is in truth a case of *post hoc ergo propter hoc* reasoning, a sort of mistaken interpretation that sees correlation as causation. The coincidence of two things in time does not necessarily mean that one has caused the other. If the theory is correct, one would expect that every encounter with death ought to obstruct positive transformation and that people cannot achieve personal psychological growth from awareness of mortality. This clearly is not supported by a sizeable body of writing and experience.

While encounters with death do not always lead to positive psychological transformation, it seems that very often they do. The literature on hospice and end-of-life care is replete with information of this sort. Existentialist psychologist Victor Frankl showed that people often, when faced with their own mortality, experience a change in values, gain a deeper appreciation of life, and come to see death as a momentous event that gives life meaning. When we remember that Frankl's theory was developed out of personal observation of fellow prisoners in Nazi camps, his claims that facing one's death has the potential to stimulate positive transformation are strikingly counter to TMT's basic thesis.

In some forms of Buddhism, the encounter with and acceptance of one's own mortality is vital to spiritual transformation. A key concept in Buddhism is the impermanence of all things, and the task facing Buddhists is to achieve comprehension and acceptance of this truth. Since the physical body is one of the most compelling aspects of life, one that gets in the way of this realization, meditation on one's own death is fundamental to achieving enlightenment.

In order to advance one's ability to detach from the material body and develop true mindfulness, in ancient times, monks often practiced contemplation of death by observing the decomposition of corpses. Today most practitioners use techniques like that described by Vietnamese Buddhist monk Thich Nhat Hanh in *Transformation and Healing: Sutra on the Four Establishments of Mindfulness*. The ninth exercise he offers in his elaboration on the Buddha's teaching is focused on imaginative contemplation of your own body after death. The meditator is to visualize the changes as the body moves from a "bloated, blue and festering" stage to skeleton to bleached and scattered bones, until there remains finally only a decomposed "pile of dust."[36] Transformation comes in and through this process of intense mortality salience.

The centrality of self-esteem to TMT also raises questions. Brad Bushman, Roy Baumeister, and others have found in research on self-esteem that high self-esteem (defined as having a favorable evaluation of oneself, whether founded in objective reality or not), not low, tends to be correlated with aggression and violence. People who have high but unstable self-esteem are especially more prone to violent action, with the highest levels of aggression found among people who have very positive and grandiose self-images. In other words, the narcissist, when undergoing threat to ego, is most likely to respond to those threats with aggression and violence. "In plainer terms, it is not so much the people who regard themselves as superior beings who are the most dangerous but, rather, those who have a strong desire to regard themselves as superior beings."[37]

Further support for this finding comes from studies of convicted serial killers and rapists. These people tend to be egotistic and narcissistic. They consciously believe that they are superior to others, and this sense of superiority is not grounded in objective reality. Baseless, and therefore fragile, high self-esteem is a strong predictor of violence and aggression.[38] These findings on the correlation between narcissism and violence are significant and will play an important role in the constructive portions of chapters 4 and 5, as we work to learn how each of us is responsible for transformation of the violent landscape of religious worlds.

Also important for the goals of this project is the problem of applicability. Is there any practical application of Terror Management Theory in everyday life? In a recent book that explores the American response to the events of 9/11, TMT theorists offer two prescriptions for amelioration of violence generated by threats to cultural worldviews: facilitation of worldview change in the direction of tolerance and reduction of "mortality salience [thinking about one's own death] in places where it has been all too salient." The creators of TMT acknowledge that these are broad and formidable claims. They do not attempt to offer concrete means for enacting them, beyond noting that things like economic security, liberal education, and moving away from politically repressive modes of government are all desirable goals.[39] These are certainly valid goals but far too general for most of us to discern our own roles in amelioration of religious violence.

Another problem arises from the fact that the safest, most secure worldview is, in the words of TMT theorists, "one with rigid, narrow, unquestioned beliefs that include a concrete depiction of the afterlife."[40] This is the very thing which makes fundamentalist religious systems attractive in a world filled with insecurity and threat. If the most rigid worldview is the most secure then the more liberal and less rigid the worldview, the more insecure individuals in such cultures should feel. Would not this insecurity born of liberal and flexible worldviews, if the theory is correct that our most basic motivator is death anxiety, necessitate activation of proximal and distal defense mechanisms that lead to the very behaviors we hope to eliminate? TMT offers no resolution here: "How secure, then, can we be? Well, without our martinis, marijuana, cocaine, Prozac . . . and so on, it appears not very."[41] So although TMT offers us resources for understanding some aspects of the human tendency to violent acts, it does not, at least in its present form, serve as a "master theory" explanatory of all aspects of human motivation—nor does it (and is not really intended to) provide tools for use at the level of the individual.

In mining social psychological approaches we have obtained some valuable resources for uncovering the roots of religious violence, particularly in terms of the impact of social groups on an individual's willingness to participate in violence against human beings. The answer to "why" religious people resort to violence in the service of transcendent goals is, at the most basic level, the same for all forms of violence and is deeply embedded in the evolutionary history of humanity. In the distant past, survival of the species depended on individual humans banding together to practice in-group niceness in the service of protection and sharing of resources. Inevitably, in-group niceness led to out-group nastiness. Adding TMT to the mix, the precariousness of survival may have resulted in a deep-seated and unconscious terror at the prospect of our own deaths. Religious ideas, as one aspect of advancing human evolution, naturally became one among many ways that groups defined themselves over against others, and the attendant death rituals and teachings about life after death worked to hold fear of death at bay. So at this level, religious violence is not much different from any other form of group violence. But were we to stop here, the implication is that there is nothing we can do in the short term of our own life spans: we must wait for evolution to work its magic.

The "how" of religious violence is, again, very similar to the way any kind of violence erupts among groups. Once a threat to the group and its worldview has been identified, various methods for coping with the threat can be tried. Often, attempts to accommodate or assimilate the other into one's own group are tried first, but should those ways fail to defuse the threat, or if the threat is perceived to be too great, elimination of the threat through any means necessary becomes the goal. Once violence comes to be seen as the most effective method for defusing the threat, moral disengagement, blaming the other, and use of euphemisms all work together with the social situation to make violence acceptable. Since authentic individual identity is contextualized by the power of the group, social constructions of violence operate powerfully to fuel acts of violence.

In terms of religious groups, things are clearly turning toward violence when certain types of beliefs converge with perceived threat to the group. Danger signs that warn of impending violence include growing insistence on the absolute nature of the group's truth claims (reification, in other words), requiring unquestioning obedience to authority and subsequent abdication of personal responsibility on the part of individual believers, and the belief that the end justifies whatever means are used to achieve it. Charles Kimball has shown that when religious leaders incorporate apocalyptic end-times rhetoric the situation becomes especially dangerous.[42] Religious ideals become perverted, morality is inverted (killing becomes a means for healing, destruction paves the way for a "New Creation," etc.), and religious narratives are revised so as to support the violence.[43] With the social and cultural background issues thoroughly examined, we are now ready to move more directly into the mind of the individual religious believer.

## NOTES

1. Rex A. Hudson, *Who Becomes a Terrorist and Why: The 1999 Government Report on Profiling Terrorists* (Guilford, CT: Lyons Press, 1999), 35.

2. Rodney Stark, *One True God: Historical Consequences of Monotheism* (Princeton, NJ: Princeton University Press, 2001), 115.

3. Fathali M. Moghaddam, *From the Terrorists' Point of View: What They Experience and Why They Come to Destroy* (Westport, CT: Praeger Security International, 2006), 46.

4. James W. Jones, "Why Does Religion Turn Violent? A Psychoanalytic Exploration of Religious Terrorism," *Psychoanalytic Review* 93, no. 2 (April 2006): 167–90.

5. "Psychoanalysis on the whole can be said to be the most comprehensive framework for analyzing religion that we presently possess." David Wulff, "How Attached Should We Be to Attachment Theory?" *International Journal for the Psychology of Religion* 16 (January 2006): 29–36.

6. Israela Silberman, "Religious Violence, Terrorism, and Peace," in *Handbook of the Psychology of Religion and Spirituality*, ed. Raymond Paloutzian and Crystal Park (New York: Guilford, 2005), 535–38.

7. Mark Jurgensmeyer, "Religion as a Cause for Terrorism," in *The Roots of Terrorism*, ed. Louise Richardson (New York: Routledge, 2006), 141–42.

8. James Waller, *Becoming Evil: How Ordinary People Commit Genocide and Mass Killing*, 2nd ed. (New York: Oxford University Press, 2007), 185.

9. Waller, *Becoming Evil*, 13.

10. Waller, *Becoming Evil*, 33–53.

11. Waller, *Becoming Evil*, 74.

12. Waller, *Becoming Evil*, 154–59.

13. Waller, *Becoming Evil*, 171–89.

14. M. Sherif, O. J. Harvey, B. J. White, W. R. Hood, and C. Sherif, *Ingroup Conflict and Cooperation: The Robber's Cave Experiment* (Norman: Oklahoma Book Exchange, 1961), cited in Waller, *Becoming Evil*, 198.

15. Philip Zimbardo, "Pathology of Imprisonment," *Society* 6 (1972): 6; quoted in Waller, *Becoming Evil*, 231.

16. Stanley Milgram, *Obedience to Authority: An Experimental View* (New York: Harper & Row, 1974).

17. Thomas Blass, *The Man Who Shocked the World* (New York: Basic Books, 2004).

18. Philip Zimbardo, *The Lucifer Effect: Understanding How Good People Turn Evil* (New York: Random House, 2007).

19. Zimbardo, *The Lucifer Effect*, 172.

20. Moghaddam, *From the Terrorists' Point of View*, 26.

21. David Wulff, *Psychology of Religion: Classic and Contemporary* (New York: John Wiley & Sons, 1997), 220–30.

22. Moghaddam, *From the Terrorists' Point of View*, 26–30, 127–28.

23. Mark Jurgensmeyer, *Terror in the Mind of God: The Global Rise of Religious Violence* (Berkeley: University of California Press, 2000), 195.

24. Jurgensmeyer, *Terror in the Mind of God*, 197.

25. Jurgensmeyer, *Terror in the Mind of God*, 214.

26. Terry McDermott, *Perfect Soldiers: The Hijackers: Who They Were, Why They Did It* (New York: Harper Collins, 2005).

27. Jonathan Yardley, "The 9/11 Hijackers," *Washington Post*, May 1, 2005, BW02.

28. Clark McCauley, "Psychological Issues in Understanding Terrorism and the Response to Terrorism," in *Psychology of Terrorism: Condensed Edition*, ed. Chris E. Stout (Westport, CT: Praeger, 2004), 43.

29. Sheldon Solomon, Jeff Greenberg, and Tom Pyszczynski, "Return of the Living Dead," *Psychological Inquiry* 8, no. 3 (1977): 59–71. See also Tom Pyszczynski, Sheldon Solomon, and Jeff Greenberg, *In the Wake of 9/11: The Psychology of Terror* (Washington, DC: American Psychological Association, 2003).

30. Jeff Greenberg, Linda Simon, Tom Pyszczynski, Sheldon Solomon, and Dan Chatel, "Terror Management and Tolerance: Does Mortality Salience Always Intensify Negative Reactions to Others Who Threaten One's Worldview?" *Journal of Personality and Social Psychology* 63 (1992): 212–20.

31. Pyszczynski et al., *In the Wake of 9/11*, 70.

32. Ray Pauloutzian, "Purpose in Life and Values Changes Following Conversion," *Journal of Personality and Social Psychology* 41 (1981): 1153–60; cited in Pyszczynski et al., *In the Wake of 9/11*, 30.

33. Martin Luther, *Luther's Works*, ed. Jaroslav Pelikan (Saint Louis, MO: Concordia, 1955), 45:229.

34. Luther, *Luther's Works*, 47:268–71.

35. Mark Muraven and Roy F. Baumeister, "Suicide, Sex, Terror, Paralysis, and Other Pitfalls of Reductionist Self-Preservation Theory," *Psychological Inquiry* 8, no. 1 (1997): 36–40.

36. Thich Nhat Hanh, *Transformation and Healing: Sutra on the Four Establishments of Mindfulness* (Berkeley, CA: Parallax Press, 1990), 56–57.

37. Brad J. Bushman and Roy F. Baumeister, "Threatened Egotism, Narcissism, Self-Esteem, and Direct and Displaced Aggression: Does Self-Love or Self-Hate Lead to Violence?" *Journal of Personality and Social Psychology* 75, no. 1 (1998): 219–29.

38. Roy F. Baumeister, *Evil: Inside Human Violence and Cruelty* (New York: Owl Books, 1999).

39. Pyszczynski et al., *In the Wake of 9/11*, 172–87.

40. Pyszczynski et al., *In the Wake of 9/11*, 197.

41. Pyszczynski et al., *In the Wake of 9/11*, 197.

42. Charles Kimball, *When Religion Becomes Evil: Five Warning Signs* (San Francisco: Harper San Francisco, 2002).

43. Robert Jay Lifton, *The Nazi Doctors: Medicalized Killing and the Psychology of Genocide* (New York: Basic Books, 1986). See also Lifton's *The Future of Immorality* (New York: Basic Books, 1987).

*Chapter Five*

# Religious Violence
# through the Lens of Psychoanalysis

Now that we have explored the cultural and social factors which are conducive to acts of religious violence, it is time to narrow the field. Our goal is discovery of the extent to which each of us holds some degree of personal responsibility for violence done in the name of religion, so we now need to study the psychological dynamics of the individual. Psychoanalytic thought is uniquely capable of providing a window into this realm. Exploration of certain themes in psychoanalysis will help illuminate the interplay among our images of God, individual egos, and collective selves, and bring to light the degree to which each of us shares responsibility for transformation of the religious landscape. In this chapter we will look first to Self and relational psychoanalytic theories to explore the dynamics at work in the individual psyche before moving to the depth and archetypal psychologies based in Carl Jung's thought. Although Jung's theories garnered much criticism from some schools of psychology during the twentieth century, his work has been quite popular among psychologists with religious affinities and has attracted a broad lay audience. This popularity in spite of the criticism is a testament to its heuristic power; in fact, "Jung anticipated many modern developments within psychoanalysis, including some aspects of self psychology," and his theory of the archetypes (to be discussed in detail below) is said to have a significance for analytic psychology "comparable to that of gravity for Newtonian physics . . . natural selection for Darwinian biology. . . . [It is] one of the most important ideas to emerge in the twentieth century."[1]

Because psychoanalysis is situated on the border between objective (laboratory or experimental) and subjective psychology (clinical), there is debate over the nature of the knowledge gained through this method. Since psychoanalysis is aimed at understanding the inner processes of one's mind, and its theories were developed within the clinical therapeutic setting, some argue that it is not scientific and therefore cannot add much of value to the conversation. What kind of knowledge is psychoanalytic knowledge? And what can it help us understand of ourselves, of the transcendent, and our relationship to it?

According to present-day conceptions, in order for a method to qualify as scientific, it must produce evidence that is falsifiable, public, and replicable. On the basis of this definition, critics say psychoanalysis is unscientific. Freudians, for example, can explain away disagreement with their theories as psychological defense mechanisms, and this makes the system unfalsifiable. There is simply no way to test the truth value of a system constructed in this manner. Since psychotherapy is conducted in privacy and under strict confidentiality guidelines, there are limits on what can be made public; if the contents of the clinical setting cannot be made fully public, replicability is restricted. An additional complication results from the individual nature of the process, which is an intense and intimate interpersonal encounter the success of which rests on the relationship between therapist and client. There is a growing body of empirical research that supports psychoanalytic theories, but as a system of thought aimed at shedding light on the human condition, psychoanalysis is not easily subjected to the scientific method.

If we think of psychoanalysis as a method of interpretation aimed at illuminating the meanings of human behavior rather than simply aimed at uncovering its causes, the question of its credentials as a science can be set aside. Psychologist and philosopher Carlo Strenger has shown that in terms of epistemology, psychoanalysis is probably much closer to historical research and legal reasoning than it is to methods employed in the natural sciences. Strenger argues that, since rationality exists outside of science, we do not need to be distracted by the question. "If the only rationally defensible way to ground empirical claims is the experimental method, most of the social sciences and humanities as well as law are nonrational disciplines and their claims are without any evidential foundations."[2]

In what follows, a number of theoretical systems will be covered. Although it is common for proponents of a particular school of psychoanalysis to vehemently dismiss the claims of other schools of thought, here we will be making use of several theorists to come to a fuller understanding of the problem of religious violence. The various approaches and theories of personality are not necessarily incompatible, in spite of the internecine battles among the diverse schools. If we think of the schools of thought as "conceptual frames" that organize phenomena in different ways, we can be cognizant of the fact that each system makes use of different methods of observation and so may provide us with different data. For example, the remainder of this chapter focuses primarily on two systems which orient the therapeutic situation in somewhat different ways: self psychology and archetypal/Jungian theories. In self psychology, the therapeutic emphasis is on creation of an empathic and emotionally safe environment which allows the client to transform damage done to the self in childhood. In archetypal/Jungian therapy, empathy between analyst and client is certainly important, but the content of sessions centers on the exploration of dreams and symbolic experience aimed at bringing into conscious awareness the underlying mechanisms (like ego inflation and projection) at work in the client's life. In attending to both of these systems, we have the opportunity to come to a richer and more complete understanding of the problem of religious violence than is possible if we were to consider the systems mutually exclusive and incompatible. Now that we have answered the question of what kind of knowledge psychoanalysis provides, we return to the question at hand: what can it help us understand of our violence-prone selves, of the transcendent, and our relationship to it?

## PSYCHOANALYSIS, RELIGION, AND VIOLENCE

Psychoanalysis is a system of thought that is based on the understanding that we humans are, for the most part, unaware of the mental processes that determine our thoughts, feelings, and behaviors, and that psychological maturity develops as we come to understand those processes. As we have seen, a number of theorists have argued that humiliation plays a role for the individual who participates in religious violence. Mark Jurgensmeyer and Jessica Stern, for example, say that young men who live in impoverished societies experience humiliation and a sense of personal emasculation. This emotion combines with other factors to bring about a situation ripe for violence. These theorists are on the right track, but in focusing on socioeconomic and political factors their analyses remain too generic and fail to explain the violence of, for example, the 9/11 terrorists. Psychoanalytic theory indicates that it is not simply social and cultural humiliation but rather a much deeper and personal sense of shame that helps explain the transition from frustrated individual to militant proponent of violence in God's name.

### Guilt, Shame, and Violence

Some of the most robust interpretive systems that evolved out of the Freudian school of psychoanalytic thought are based in Heinz Kohut's (1913–1981) self psychology. Kohut brought together Freudian "drive" theory, which posits that we are motivated to act by certain innate drives or instincts (e.g., *Eros* and *Thanatos*, for Freud), and a more interpersonal, relational model of

self-development. One major difference between Freud and Kohut on the issues pertinent to this discussion is that Freud focused on guilt, whereas Kohut saw the narcissism-shame dynamic as primary. The distinction between
shame and guilt is important to the dynamics underlying violence.

Guilt feelings tend to be associated with acts we have committed; guilt is
associated "with the 'external' evaluation of transgression."[3] In the experience of guilt, our thoughts run along the lines of "how could I have *done*
*that?*" with the focus on the action itself. Guilt actually tends to inhibit expression of hostility because it is connected to an internalized sense of justice;
we sense we have done wrong and deserve punishment. Since we know we
have done wrong, as the theory goes, we are not as likely to commit yet another transgression through striking out violently.

Shame is an emotion associated with self-judgment; it is not about being at
fault but rather about lacking something. If shamed, we feel exposed and
think "how could *I* have done that?" Since shame is connected with feelings
of weakness and inadequacy it is more likely to stimulate aggression.[4] As Eric
Erickson put it, when shamed, "one is completely exposed . . . visible and not
ready to be visible . . . [shame] is essentially rage turned against the self. He
who is shamed . . . would like to destroy the eyes of the world."[5] Shame can
also be understood interpersonally as arising when our very basic expectations of significant others are shown to have been wrong. This is experienced
as a betrayal of trust, which leads to a feeling of foolishness for having trusted
the untrustworthy one and anger at having been betrayed. The sense of shame
is more self-referential than guilt; shame involves a negative evaluation of the
self as inferior, whereas in guilt the focus is on action, with the self only indirectly found wanting.

## Origins of Shame and Narcissism

Kohut believed that narcissism and shame are universals in human experience
and that these internal experiences are vital to the formation of a healthy
sense of self. In self psychology and later interpretations, like relational psychoanalytic thought, the human infant is thought to start life in a state of self-
absorption called primary narcissism. We are born narcissists, in other words,
and some degree of self-love is necessary in order to be able to negotiate the
path to psychological maturity. When the caregiving environment provides
appropriately empathetic responding to an infant's needs, which includes
some frustration when the caregiver fails to meet every need, the child is able
to develop the capacity to take care of herself emotionally.

The original state of primary narcissism gradually breaks down as the infant develops internalized psychic structures that help to recreate the sense of

idyllic existence in which one is the "center of the universe." Out of this process evolve two narcissistic psychic structures, the grandiose self and the idealized parent imago or image. This duality, "I am perfect" and "you are perfect, but I am a part of you," in an ideal situation preserves the illusion of perfection only long enough to allow disappointment to gradually lead to more realistic assessments of oneself and one's parents.[6] Under optimum conditions, the two narcissistic aspects are integrated gradually, with the grandiose self giving way to a realistic degree of self-esteem and goal-directedness. The idealized parental image will gradually be transmuted into the superego; these changes result in a kind of "bipolar self" which exists in a state of tension between ambitions and ideals.[7]

Even under optimum conditions, shame is experienced as the sense of self evolves. Shame is a normal response to the failure of important others to respond to the infant's needs appropriately. It centers on the sense of vulnerability. Shame can be seen "as narcissism in the infant that is not responded to. The absence of the expected response in the mother or parent triggers in the infant a wish to hide its needs, to be ashamed of wanting them gratified."[8]

Idealization and realistic assessment of oneself and others are in tension throughout life. In fact, narcissistic idealizing is necessary so that we can emotionally invest in others; reality testing helps to keep narcissism grounded.[9] If we fail to develop healthy self structures (which Kohut called "selfobjects") the outcome is a pathological form of narcissism. When shame arises due to narcissistic needs being inadequately received by the environment, the first psychological defense is denial of need, distancing from others, and turning inward to substitute self-care. When rejection is extreme and continual, it becomes necessary to defend the self. Driven by object hunger and dependency, the person who has suffered continual failure in early relationships must develop self-protective psychological mechanisms to avoid further injury. This can be accomplished through a variety of means, including isolation, power seeking, taking a righteous stance in relation to others, and rage.

Compensation through turning inward can develop into the extreme of pathological narcissism wherein the individual believes he needs no one.[10] In terms of power as a defense against shame, the narcissistically wounded individual can make use of it either directly through attempts to exert power over others or indirectly by controlling others through helplessness. Helplessness is most often seen in small group dynamics, like family situations where dependency can be a potent manipulative tool. Power seeking, the form of power most pertinent to our agenda here, can be utilized as a direct compensation for feelings of inferiority that arise in the face of shame; the more power one can exert over others the less susceptible she will feel to experiencing more shame.

A common response to shame is the experience of self-righteousness driven by the need to be correct as a defense against feelings of inferiority. If one is convinced of the rightness of one's position then one is not accountable for events. By extension, self-righteousness makes room for blaming others for the situation at hand: "The claim of being in the right depends on the ability to locate the problem elsewhere." This maneuver locates power in the hands of the self-righteous one and can lead to retaliatory moves.[11] Here, shame and guilt work together to produce aggression: Shame → guilt → retaliation. This mechanism may be the driving force behind the use of violence in response to direct challenges to our worldviews.

Another means of defense against shame is the experience of narcissistic rage, a primitive and irrational response to injured self-esteem. This "prototype of human aggression" is devoid of empathy and driven by the need to protect the self from further psychic harm. Someone who develops this response pattern does not recognize the other "as a center of independent initiative with whom one happens to be at cross purposes" but rather is seen as "a flaw in a narcissistically perceived reality . . . a recalcitrant part of an expanded self."[12] Narcissistic rage is especially problematic since it can become disconnected from the original source of shame. This rage can develop into a pattern of responding, a kind of indiscriminate reaction to various stimuli that are unrelated to the source.[13]

The mature self is not free of narcissism and the need for idealized self objects. In maturity, the person has developed the ability to identify empathic and appropriately responsive selfobjects that mirror, or reflect back, a sense of value or worth. Instead of being driven by object hunger and dependency, the healthy, mature individual is capable of empathy; has a sense of humor, curiosity, and creativity; and accepts the fact of her own mortality.[14] But if narcissism is a basic psychic energy, then how can a person accept her own mortality? This is where religion comes into play.

## Religion, Cosmic Narcissism, and Shame

According to Kohut we can work through and transform the narcissistic energies of childhood grandiosity through the process he called "transmuting internalization." This is possible when the self is able to engage selfobjects empathetically and at the same time learns to tolerate failures of the empathetic bonds.[15] Over the course of a lifetime, the interplay of these experiences can lead to a more positive global narcissism which he called "cosmic narcissism." This cosmic narcissism is rooted in the primordial experience of identity with the mother but is experienced as a kind of self-transcendence in which the person participates in a "supraindividual and timeless existence." It is a rare achievement, "the enduring, creative result of the steadfast activities of an autonomous ego" that is characterized by "quasi-religious solemnity."[16] What happens, in other words, is that the self comes to be identified with all creation, and consequently the cosmos is now itself a sacred realm within which empathy is expressed and experienced. Narcissism and idealization are in this way central to religious experience: "The relationship of the true believer to his God . . . in which the figure of the perfect and omnipotent God, with whom the powerless and humble believer wants to merge, corresponds to the ancient omnipotent self-object, the idealized parent imago."[17]

James W. Jones points out that there is continuity between the psychology underlying religion and other aspects of life. Religious experience and denotation of something as sacred very often mean seeing old things in new ways. To experience something as sacred is not unlike other forms of idealization; in fact, "religions seem to require idealization as a pre-requisite for commitment." In a sense, that which we call sacred can be understood as "the intensification or refocusing of the normal idealizations of everyday life.[18] But the idealization process is ambivalent since it potentially brings about a positive transformation in the personality and can also be used by religious leaders to encourage infantile states of dependence.

In his 2002 book, *Terror and Transformation*, Jones argued that religious fanaticism is fueled by idealization. According to relational and self psychologies, we must idealize objects and others in order to develop and maintain healthy selves, and religion is a prime source of suitable objects. Unfortunately, religious leaders who insist on belief that a particular view is the absolute truth tend to split the world into good versus evil, us versus them, saved versus damned. Splitting is a psychological defense mechanism that first comes into play when the caregiver fails to meet an infant's needs. In order to feel safe and maintain the idealized parent image, the world is "split" into the all-good external parent and the internalized bad-self. This type of interaction can lead to infantile dependence by members on the leaders and feed into the development of violent fanaticism. Jones makes an important point in noting that this psychological splitting "parallels exactly the dichotomy between the sacred and profane" seen in so many religious systems.[19]

Jones has recently revised his thesis on the causes of religious violence to include the mechanism of shame and humiliation. In the 2006 essay "Why Does Religion Turn Violent?" Jones says, "It is not idealization alone that is central to the psychology of religious violence but an idealized object that is also a source of shame and humiliation." He argues that when religious leaders manipulate textual interpretation to support punishing and vengeful views of the divine, internal mechanisms of shame and humiliation are "hooked" into a psychological cycle which can end in violence. The archaic need for union with the punitive idealized Other overpowers empathic personal connections and engenders splitting into all-good versus all-bad domains of thought: "Idealizing the other [whether it be God or a human being] means inevitably denigrating oneself." This denigration of self can then be projected outward against the demonized Other in acts of violence.[20]

While all the major schools of psychoanalytic thought agree that narcissism and its attendant grandiosity make up a basic human problem, some are critical of self and relational psychologies because it is not entirely clear whether or not we ought to understand "transmuting internalization" as the total transformation of narcissism and infantile grandiosity.[21] Another more significant issue arises in understanding just what is at the basis of the developing self. Jones says that while all psychoanalytic systems agree that human character is the expression of deeper forces, in relational psychology "human experience is structured around the establishment and maintenance of connections with others," and it is the nature of our relationships, not "some impersonal biological drive" or instinct, that determines the quality of our experiences.[22] This tendency to so divorce human experience from biology has become problematic in light of evolutionary psychology. The development of humans as a species is a dual process of biological and cultural evolution; the human need for interpersonal relatedness arises out of biological and cultural influences. While the characteristics which make humans truly unique may be shaped more by historical and ontogenetic than biological factors, the truth remains that human beings are still very much the product of biological evolution. In fact, since the 1980s evolutionary theorists have postulated the existence of evolved neuropsychic tendencies, mental modules, or response propensities which are responsible for the universals in human cultures.[23]

In light of these issues, the psychoanalytic system that promises to be most fruitful for our endeavor here is archetypal psychology, which is based on the work of Carl G. Jung. First, while Jung would agree for the most part with Kohut's explanation of the self as shaped by narcissism and idealization and also with Jones's explanation of causative factors in religious violence, he would find self and relational psychologies lacking. This is so because in their eagerness to highlight the impact of relationship on the development of the self they have denied any connection to biology and thus to our evolutionary past. The claim that we do not come into the world with any sort of a priori self structures or aggressive instincts, and so on, would be quite problematic for Jung, as it is for anyone influenced today by evolutionary theory. Jones is critical of Jung for having offered something like a "psychological ontology . . . in which the unconscious becomes the universal ground from which individual selfhood emerges." Echoing much of twentieth-century psychology's rhetoric regarding archetypal psychology, he says that because Jungian thought implies there are forces at work outside the individual ego which "bring healing and wholeness" this makes Jung's psychology "a theology in psychological dress."[24]

Today, however, criticism is being leveled against systems based in Kohut's thought precisely because they lack grounding and see the self as developing through an unsupported process of accretion as selfobject relationships are internalized. To what do the internalized selfobjects attach? Self psychology offers no explanation. Although it would be premature to claim that science has vindicated Jung on this, since the 1980s discoveries in ethology, evolutionary psychology, and anthropology have made it apparent that Jung's claims for an a priori structural principle in the psyche were on target.

In an essay comparing Jung and Kohut, Lionel Corbett demonstrates that Jung's work supports and advances Kohut's theory of the self. Through the metaphor of clay sculpting this is nicely illustrated. If we think of the self as a dynamic sculpture, with Jung's theory of the self making up the wire armature and Kohut's theory the clay, then Jung's self provides the framework and ground onto which Kohut's self can be attached. Without the wire armature, Kohut's self is merely formless clay; without the clay, Jung's self remains too generic.[25]

Jung's psychology is more robust not only because it is quite compatible with evolutionary thought. Jungian theories are preferable for this project because of archetypal psychology's heuristic power. Jung's work has had a sustained following among analysts who find his work enriches other systems and therapeutic approaches. Christian clergy have found Jungian and archetypal psychology to be a rich source of material for enhancing the lives of their congregations. Many intelligent lay people have discovered archetypal psychology's power for personal transformation through the writings of psychologists like James Hillman, Thomas Moore, John Sanford, and Robert A. Johnson, among others. Jung's theories speak to a wide variety of professionals and lay people, perhaps much more so than any other single system of psychoanalytic thought. This is so because these theories resonate powerfully with the lived experience of many. Taken as an interpretive lens, archetypal psychology can help us construct a solid foundation on which to stand as we address the problem of religious violence.

## THE JUNGIAN SELF, EGO INFLATION, AND VIOLENCE

In Jungian thought, the development of the self is more expansive than self and relational psychologies allow. Jung believed that human consciousness is an extraordinary evolutionary achievement, albeit a precarious one. People in the present day are only slightly more able to maintain consciousness than the earliest humans, as is demonstrated by the tendencies among us toward mental illness, mass movements like Nazism, and warfare. Because so much of human experience and motivation remains outside of conscious awareness even among modern human beings, the unconscious and its contents play a central role in Jungian thought. According to this framework, psychological health and wholeness cannot be achieved without careful attention to the unconscious. The individual psyche is not just a product of personal experience; there is a "pre-personal" or transpersonal aspect to it due to its origins in the evolutionary history of humankind. This transpersonal dimension is revealed in universal images and patterns like those common to myths and religions the world over, and it helps to account for the power of situational factors to transform normal men and women into genocidal monsters.

## The Unconscious Mind

Individual mental experience occurs on three levels: the conscious, personal unconscious, and collective unconscious. Consciousness is an adaptive accomplishment, the full achievement of which is the (perhaps asymptotic) goal of human existence. The unconscious, as the source of the instinctual forces of the psyche, is very powerful and can overwhelm consciousness if we are not vigilant. The personal unconscious lies just beneath conscious awareness and is made up of memories, sense impressions, and repressed material accumulated during a person's lifetime.

The concept of the collective unconscious came about as a result of Jung's research into the similarities he and a colleague noted among families who participated in his research on the Word Association Test. The results of tests showed an uncanny commonality to associations that seemed to be more significant than could be accounted for by simple familial or cultural influences. On the basis of these discoveries, Jung postulated the existence of collective structures that influence individuals in the formation of knowledge.[26] Over the course of time, as he worked with clients on their dreams and explored mythologies of the world, he began to suspect there must be some universal aspect of the human mind, perhaps the remnants of the long evolutionary process. His theory of the collective unconscious serves as a way to conceptualize the shared unconscious structures that many believe must exist, given the commonality of images that appear in human dreams, myths, and fairy tales across time and cultures.

Defined more formally, the collective unconscious is the realm of supraindividual psychic activity, a repository of the universal "ancestral heritage of possibilities of representation" containing the "whole spiritual heritage of [hu]mankind's evolution, born anew in the brain structure of every individual." It is the source of the archetypes, which are forms or categories that regulate the forces of our psyches.[27]

Even though Jungians at times reify the concept, archetypes are not things or discrete entities. They are best understood as "unconscious images of the instincts themselves," patterns of instinctual behavior that arise from the collective unconscious. They influence perception and emotional experience, operating something like genetically encoded possibilities. As universal motifs or "pre-existent forms," traces of ancestral psychology that account for the common themes in our dreams and myths, archetypes are very important to our understanding of the processes that lead ordinary people to commit extraordinary acts of cruelty and violence.[28] Although Jung wrote of many different archetypes, the most important ones for our purposes here are the Self and the Shadow. We will explore the archetypes and their connection to religious violence in greater depth shortly, but first, more about the development of the individual psyche.

## The Developing Self and Ego Inflation

As the reader may have already noted, the Jungian theoretical portrayal of the human psyche's structure is a bit more complex than Kohut's or Jones's theories. "Self" is a superordinate term for Jung that refers to the original state out of which the individual ego is born.[29] The Self (when referring to the archetype it is written with a capital *S*) is the most important of the archetypal conceptions in Jungian thought. Like Kohut and Jones, Jung thought the self is ultimately an "unknowable essence."[30] The Self can be thought of as the seat of objective identity, the shared core reality of what it means to be human, whereas the ego is the seat of subjective identity. It may be helpful to think of the self (small "s") in relational psychology as equivalent to the Jungian ego; there is no conceptual equivalent to Jung's Self in the other theories.

At birth, the human infant's experience of the world is conceptualized to be a state of more-or-less undifferentiated wholeness. At this earliest stage of life the ego, or center of conscious personality, is nascent: "The Self is born, but the ego is made; and in the beginning all is Self."[31] Although the reasons given for this differ from relational psychology, Jungians also see the original state of the infant in terms of narcissism and grandiosity, which they call ego inflation. Whether we call the basic problem infantile grandiosity (Kohut), the omnipotence illusion (D. W. Winnicott), or ego inflation (Jung), psychoanalysts agree on the type of care that must be given for healthy mental development.

Early in life, the caregiving environment should be one in which the infant's needs are very nearly always met. Over time need gratification should be delayed, with a gradual increase in optimal failures so that the infant learns he is not a god, does not control the world, and is not the center of the universe. In Jungian terms, this process involves the gradual differentiation of the ego (center of subjective identity) from the Self (center of objective human reality). The following diagram is an attempt to illustrate this process of progressive differentiation:[32]

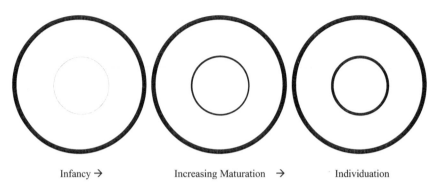

Infancy →      Increasing Maturation →      Individuation

**Figure 5.1. Process of Progressive Differentiation**

In the diagram, the small inner circle represents the ego and the larger outer circle is the Self. The Self, as the matrix within and out of which the ego has its existence, is portrayed as unchanged across the life span since it is essentially unknowable. Ideally, as the environment provides challenges to the ego inflation resulting from undefined ego boundaries that allow for identification with the Self, the ego gradually becomes more distinguishable from the Self. In complete individuation, full consciousness (a state perhaps only achieved by truly unique people like Jesus or the Buddha), the ego would be clearly distinguishable from the Self, while its center and the center of the Self remain identical.

Because the Self is the center and source of being, when the ego is completely fused or identified with the Self, it experiences itself as a kind of deity. This is ego inflation. Encounters with reality inevitably challenge the ego's selfish assumptions. If this does not happen to a sufficient degree, grandiosity, at least, and mental illness, at worst, can be the end result. The severely mentally ill person may, for example, have delusions that he is some great figure from history, like George Washington or Jesus. Paranoid psychoses often include "ideas of reference" in which the ill person is convinced that independent actual events are actually "referencing" them. (I once cared for a patient who was convinced that Walter Cronkite, the news reporter, came on the television each evening to send secret messages of love to the man's wife!)

Development of a healthy human self occupies the entire lifespan of an individual. The task of our early years is centered on achieving gradual differentiation of the ego from its ground in the Self. In later years the task is to undergo a kind of relativizing of the ego in which we seek to become cognizant of the contents of the unconscious and integrate them into consciousness, a process called individuation (to be addressed more fully shortly).

Believing oneself to be the center of the universe is normal in early childhood, but if it persists into adulthood this confusion of ego and Self is an unhealthy and potentially dangerous inflation of the ego. The Self is the "sum total of conscious and unconscious existence"; Jung sometimes referred to it, for reasons which will become clearer as we proceed, as the "God within us." So if we do not successfully emerge from childhood with a more realistic and balanced ego-Self relation, we will be prone to living out the inflation in destructive ways. This failure to recenter the personality in adulthood often manifests in the context of religion. Claims to know the mind of God or to have the absolute and exclusive truth are examples. To assert that one knows God and that this knowledge is absolute and objective is a serious psychological mistake because what has happened here is that the ego has become identified with the archetypal Self.

When the ego confuses itself with the Self, people are prone to claiming universal validity for experiences that are only valid for the individual, as happens in religions which insist that since theirs is the only legitimate path to salvation all humanity must accept it.[33] The end result of this sort of thinking tends to be conflict with those who do not share the experience or whose beliefs tell them otherwise. As Jung put it, "If the ego is dissolved in identification with the self, it gives rise to a sort of nebulous superman with a puffed-up ego."[34] This experience of "universal validity—'godlikeness'—which completely ignores all differences" leads to attempts to "force the demands of [one's] own unconscious upon others."[35] When combined with issues that arise from our failure to attend to another of the powerful archetypal forces, the Shadow, this phenomenon can make human beings very dangerous.

Placing Jung's work in its historical context will help us to better grasp the importance of this concept.

## Jung in Context

Jung (1875–1961) was Swiss and the son of a Reformed Church Christian pastor. He was fascinated by religious and mythological questions from a very early age. After studies in archeology, philosophy, Christian historical theology, and mythology he finally settled on medicine and became a physician in 1902. His first research endeavor involved the word association studies mentioned previously. These experiments led to his discovery of what he called "complexes," unconscious groupings of impulses or associated ideas which impact thought and behavior, and brought him to the attention of Freud, with whom he worked closely for several years. In spite of Freud's having, as he put it, "adopted [Jung] as an eldest son, anointing [Jung] as my successor and crown prince,"[36] the relationship ended abruptly in 1912 over theoretical differences.

Their parting of ways came about because Jung thought Freud was too negative in his understanding of human nature and overly concerned with sexuality
as the root of all psychological problems. The break was very difficult for Jung,
and he underwent a period of uncertainty and psychological distress which
came to a head with the outbreak of World War I in 1914. As a Swiss citizen,
he was in a position of political and military neutrality, but psychologically and
emotionally he suffered a long period of what he called "darkness" which only
dissipated after the end of the war. Professionally this spell of darkness was
fruitful since it led to his development of the basic structure of his psychological theory during the last years of this period.

The first half of the twentieth century was a time of tremendous change in
the Western world. Political, social, and economic upheaval was ongoing.
Rising nationalism had led to the outbreak of World War I, and the economic
repercussions of that war fed into the social and political trends that eventuated in World War II. Jung is in many ways a reflection of the more global
forces at work in the Western world during this time. Secularization, modernization, rapid and transformative technological developments including
weapons with enough power to destroy all life, and mass sociopolitical movements all impacted his theoretical development.

A hallmark of modern societies is the move toward pluralization, individual autonomy, and separation of private from public morality. This process
had been set in motion in the Western world by the nineteenth century's industrial revolution and is reflected in Freud's theory of oedipal conflict. Peter
Homans says that, prior to the industrial revolution, fathers were more "present" in the lives of their children, but as a consequence of it fathers were removed from the family in such a way as to set up psychological conflict between parent and offspring. Tradition was being overturned, and so concepts
of psychological conflict between autonomy and inclusion were therefore
central to Freud's thought, whereas they served as merely the beginning for
Jung. Rather than jettison tradition in favor of modernity, Jung sought to integrate them into a single process, which he called individuation. Jung's archetypes of the collective unconscious represent the core of tradition. His Traditional or "Archaic Man" is prone to dependence and exclusion, not
autonomy and inclusiveness. The individuation process involves the break-
down of the persona, which allows emergence of archetypal material from the
collective unconscious, differentiation of the ego from the archetypes, and the
gradual integration of these energies. The end result of the process is "establishment of the self as a 'midpoint' between the ego and the collective."[37]

The twentieth century marks the beginning of modernization that continues
to the present day. Jung's work, like all scholarship, is very much shaped by
the circumstances within which it developed. Homans's analysis of Jung

helps us see that Jung is very much a thinker for our time. Jung's self both assimilates and renounces the past. His is a revitalized interpretation of the healthy person as a member of a new kind of community that is not derivative of projections of the collective Shadow but rather is shaped by traits brought into being by the individuation process.

## The Shadow and Violence

The process of individuation is an ongoing one aimed at bringing into conscious awareness the forces at work in the unconscious. The most important of these forces are those related to the Shadow. The Shadow archetype represents the undeveloped and unacceptable qualities (positive and negative) of the personality. The Shadow's "nature can in large measure be inferred from the contents of the personal unconscious,"[38] although it has effects at both personal and collective levels. Because it takes shape in personal and collective archetypal forms, the Shadow exerts a powerful influence in human experience; for this reason, in Jungian therapy problems related to it are usually the first, and often most difficult, to be addressed.

> The shadow is a moral problem that challenges the whole ego personality, for no one can become conscious of the shadow without considerable moral effort. To become conscious of it involves recognizing the dark aspects of the personality as present and real. This act [becoming aware of one's Shadow] is the essential condition for any self-knowledge, and it therefore, as a rule, meets with considerable resistance.[39]

Confronting the darker side of our own natures in the quest for self-knowledge inevitably questions ego-Self identification and its attendant ego inflation. Challenges to the "puffed up ego" are perceived as deeply threatening to the very structure of our selves. This dynamic accounts for the recalcitrance of our unconscious in facing up to the objectionable aspects of our personalities which we attempt to deny by relegating them to the Shadow.

Dealing with the Shadow is quite difficult since it disturbs the uneasy equilibrium of ego-Self identification and calls into question our self-images. Conflict between Shadow and ego can become intense and if not reconciled results in a kind of neurotic splitting in the personality such that the person seems to be at war with himself. This phenomenon is attested to in the myths, literature, and cultural expressions of the world: Robert Louis Stevenson's tale of Dr. Jekyll and Mr. Hyde was a favorite example for Jung. Other examples abound from ancient to modern times, including the German folk legend of the doppelgänger, Dostoyevsky's *The Double*, Superman's evil twin Bizarro, and Venom, Spiderman's evil twin.

One of the most difficult roadblocks to attaining consciousness of the personal Shadow's contents takes the form of our psychological projections onto others:

> Although, with insight and good will, the shadow can to some extent be assimilated into the conscious personality, experience shows that there are certain features which offer the most obstinate resistance to moral control and prove almost impossible to influence. These resistances are usually bound up with *projections*, which are not recognized as such . . . because the cause of [the problems] appears to lie, beyond all possible doubt, in the *other person.*[40]

Not all projection is necessarily bad, since positive Shadow projections can enhance affection among people, but the person who projects the majority of her negative Shadow outward is certain to interpret the world in very negative terms. Negative projections lead to beliefs that the world is filled with people who exhibit the person's (or group's) un-owned characteristics—*they* are wrong, evil, and so on, while *I* am good, victimized by *them*.

At this juncture, we see that psychoanalytic theories agree that unresolved ego inflation or narcissism is at the core of human violence. They further agree that challenges to one's grandiosity make the situation ripe for aggression against the offending other. Kohut and Jones see shame as ultimately the motivating emotion; this does not, however, constitute a significant departure from Jungian thought. Although shame is not specifically addressed in Jungian works except as it operates within the constellation of emotions aroused by confrontation with the Shadow, the shame-humiliation dynamic is part of the process which leads to projection of unacceptable psychic contents onto others.

Projection allows us to maintain the ego inflation born of ego-Self identification. Sadly, once personal projection occurs, it can be easily taken up into a collective process, the end result of which has often been violence in the name of our gods. When one refuses to accept any ownership for Shadow projections it can lead to a more serious manifestation of it as an archetype of the collective unconscious, about which more will be said in the next chapter, since it relates directly to Jungian interpretation of religion and of our God-images. It suffices at this point in our discussion to note that Shadow projections of the collective cultural unconscious are the root cause of warfare. Examples of recent manifestations of this dynamic include Adolph Hitler's power and the success of the Nazi ideology among Germans, the Taliban's control of Afghanistan, Osama bin Laden's proclamation of jihad against the United States, and American support of the "war against terror."

For Jung, the God-image is an expression of not who/what God is but rather who/what *we* are: religious imagery is "the phenomenology of the objective psyche." Images of the transcendent, no matter the form they take, are manifestations of the collective self, which is "a transpersonal center shared by a whole body of humanity."[41] We will unpack this statement shortly, but first it will be helpful to explore a bit about his epistemological premises. Then will we be in a position to take the final step with Jung into what has been called a "psychological ethics" that uncovers the relationship between the individual human psyche and the progressive transformation of the God-image in human history.[42] In following this path we will reach a deeper understanding of religious violence and perhaps be better prepared to take steps toward its eventual amelioration.

## NOTES

1. The first quote is from Lionel Corbett, "Kohut and Jung: A Comparison of Theory and Therapy," in *Self Psychology: Comparisons and Contrasts*, ed. Douglas W. Detrick and Susan B. Detrick (Hillsdale, NJ: Analytic Press, 1989), www.findingstone.com/professionals/monographs/kohutandjung.htm (accessed August 7, 2007). The second quote is from Anthony Stevens, "The Archetypes," in *The Handbook of Jungian Psychology: Theory, Practice, and Applications*, ed. Renos K. Papadopoulos (London: Routledge, 2006), 74–93.

2. Carlo Strenger, *Between Hermeneutics and Science: An Essay on the Epistemology of Psychoanalysis* (Madison, CT: International Universities Press, 1991), 146–51.

3. Benjamin Kilborne, "Fields of Shame: Anthropologists Abroad," *Ethos* 20, no. 2 (June 1992): 231–32.

4. John Patton, *Is Human Forgiveness Possible?* (Nashville: Abingdon Press, 1985), 43–46.

5. Eric H. Erickson, *Childhood and Society* (New York: W. W. Norton, 1950), 252–53; quoted in Patton, *Is Human Forgiveness Possible?* 47.

6. Heinz Kohut, *The Analysis of the Self* (New York: International Universities Press, 1971), 25–28.

7. Heinz Kohut, *The Restoration of the Self* (New York: International Universities Press, 1977), 180.

8. Kilborne, "Fields of Shame," 239.

9. James W. Jones, *Terror and Transformation: The Ambiguity of Religion in Psychoanalytic Perspective* (New York: Routledge, 2002), 21.

10. Patton, *Is Human Forgiveness Possible?* 56–57.

11. Patton, *Is Human Forgiveness Possible?* 93–101.

12. Heinz Kohut, "Narcissism and Narcissistic Rage," in *The Psychoanalytic Study of the Child* (New York: Quadrangle Press, 1972), 377–86.

13. Patton, *Is Human Forgiveness Possible?* 108–9.

14. David Wulff, *Psychology of Religion Classic and Contemporary*, 2nd ed. (New York: John Wiley & Sons, 1997), 356.

15. Heinz Kohut, *How Does Analysis Cure?* (Chicago: Chicago University Press, 1984), 70.

16. Heinz Kohut, "Forms and Transformations of Narcissism," *Journal of the American Psychoanalytic Association* 14 (1966): 243–72.

17. Kohut, *Analysis of the Self*, 106.

18. Jones, *Terror and Transformation*, 60–65.

19. Jones, *Terror and Transformation*, 55, 77–78.

20. James W. Jones, "Why Does Religion Turn Violent? A Psychoanalytic Exploration of Religious Terrorism," *Psychoanalytic Review* 93, no. 2 (April 2006): 167–90.

21. Robert L. Monroe, *Facing the Dragon: Confronting Personal and Spiritual Grandiosity* (Wilmette, IL: Chiron Publications, 2003), 133–35.

22. Jones, *Terror and Transformation*, 4–5.

23. Stevens, "The Archetypes," 83.

24. Jones, *Terror and Transformation*, 99–101.

25. Corbett, "Kohut and Jung."

26. Renos K. Papadopoulos, "Jung's Epistemology and Methodology," in *The Handbook of Jungian Psychology: Theory, Practice, and Applications*, ed. Renos K. Papadopoulos (London: Routledge, 2006), 7–53.

27. C. G. Jung, *The Structure and Dynamics of the Psyche*, in *The Collected Works*, trans. R. F. C. Hull, ed. H. Read, M. Fordham, G. Adler, and W. McGuire, vol. 8, Bollingen Series (Princeton, NJ: Princeton University Press, 1953–1983), paras. 283–342.

28. C. G. Jung, *The Archetypes and the Collective Unconscious*, in *The Collected Works*, trans. R. F. C. Hull, ed. H. Read, M. Fordham, G. Adler, and W. McGuire, vol. 9/1, Bollingen Series 20 (Princeton, NJ: Princeton University Press, 1968/1980), paras. 87–110.

29. Michael Fordham, *New Developments in Analytical Psychology* (London: Routledge & Kegan Paul, 1957).

30. C. G. Jung, *Two Essays in Analytical Psychology*, in *The Collected Works*, trans. R. F. C. Hull, ed. H. Read, M. Fordham, G. Adler, and W. McGuire, vol. 7, Bollingen Series 20 (Princeton, NJ: Princeton University Press, 1966).

31. Edward F. Edinger, *Ego and Archetype: Individuation and the Religious Function of the Psyche* (Boston: Shambala, 1992), 7.

32. Edinger, *Ego and Archetype*, 5, depicts the process using circles that gradually become separated. I believe this is misleading, since the Self is the totality, or ground. Depiction of the process as one of gradually increasing ego definition is more true to Jung's intent.

33. C. G. Jung, *Letters*, trans. R. F. C. Hull, ed. Gerhard Adler and Aniela Jaffé, Bollingen Series 95: 1–2 (Princeton, NJ: Princeton University Press, 1973), 376; quoted in Edward F. Edinger, *The New God-Image: A Study of Jung's Key Letters Concerning the Evolution of the Western God-Image*, ed. Diane D. Cordic and Charles Yates (Wilmette, IL: Chiron Publications, 1996), 10.

34. C. G. Jung, *The Structure and Dynamics of the Psyche*, para. 430.

35. C. G. Jung, "Relations between the Ego and the Unconscious," in *The Portable Jung*, ed. Joseph Campbell (New York: Penguin Press, 1928/1976), 99.

36. Letter from Freud to Jung, April 16, 1909, printed in C. G. Jung, *Memories, Dreams, Reflections*, trans. Richard and Clara Winston, ed. Aniela Jaffé (New York: Vintage Books, 1961/1989), 361.

37. Peter Homans, *Jung in Context: Modernity and the Making of Psychology* (Chicago: University of Chicago Press, 1979/1995), 135–42.

38. C. G. Jung, "The Shadow," in *The Collected Works*, trans. R. F. C. Hull, ed. H. Read, M. Fordham, G. Adler, and W. McGuire, vol. 9/2, Bollingen Series (Princeton, NJ: Princeton University Press, 1953–1983), para. 13.

39. Jung, "The Shadow," para. 14.

40. Jung, "The Shadow," para. 16.

41. Edinger, *The New God-Image*, xxi.

42. Edinger, *The New God-Image*, xxii. On Jung's "psychological ethics" see 84ff.

## Chapter Six

# Knowing God, Knowing Ourselves

Since the constructive portion of this work regarding the root causes of religious violence is grounded in archetypal psychology, it will be necessary in this chapter to explore some of the philosophical and theological underpinnings of Jung's work, and in order to do this, we will first need to attend to the problem of mistaken interpretations.[1] Misunderstandings of archetypal psychology have been problematic in the past partly because some "Jungians" have developed a cultish mode of speaking and writing; one does not need to deify Jung in order to benefit from his work. Other reasons for misunderstanding arise because Jung's writings incorporate themes and terminology from philosophy, theology, mythology, Eastern and Western religions, Gnosticism, and alchemy. He was a brilliant man and, like many truly gifted intellectuals, not always able to clearly communicate his synthesis of massive amounts of information. One of the most common and regrettable errors made in reading Jung involves misreading his writings on religion and God-images.

For Jung, our God-images cannot be assumed to tell us anything about God *in se*. There is much information to be gained from examination of our conceptions of the Transcendent, but that information is about who and what *we* are, not about the actual God. Jung frequently attempted to clarify this issue in his essays and correspondence; numerous citations are possible, but his intent is clearly summed up in this statement made in a letter: "I make no metaphysical assertions. My standpoint is purely empirical and deals with the psychology of such assertions."[2] While it is debatable how successfully and consistently he avoided metaphysics, it was nevertheless his intent to do so as much as possible. He believed it possible to separate metaphysical from psychological assertions about God because of his philosophical inclinations, which were shaped by his admiration for the German philosopher Immanuel Kant (1724–1804). Jung believed Kant had established the foundation upon which a scientific understanding of the human psyche could be built. Expressing his appreciation for Kant's epistemology, Jung wrote that Kant's theory of knowledge was the entryway to a new level of comprehension, and "on that threshold minds go their separate ways: those that have understood Kant, and the others that cannot follow him."[3] In the following excursus on those aspects of philosophy and theology that were most influential for Jung, we examine Kant's epistemology and Friedrich Schleiermacher's response to it (for reasons explained below) so as to develop a full appreciation of the conceptual framework within which Jung operated. Readers with little interest in philosophical speculation may skim over this material and return to more careful reading with "Jung's Epistemology and Religious Experience."

## EXCURSUS: KANT, SCHLEIERMACHER, AND THE LIMITS OF HUMAN KNOWLEDGE

Kant's philosophy is quite complex, and portions of it are said to be nearly incomprehensible even for academic philosophers.[4] It is possible, however, to convey the gist here of at least those portions so important to Jung and archetypal psychologies of religion. Kant developed his theory of knowledge as a mediating response to the claims of empiricists, for whom knowledge is derived from sense experience alone, and the rationalists, for whom reason can provide genuinely objective knowledge which is uncontaminated by experience. Kant accepted that each of these approaches contained some truth but thought neither was entirely correct when taken on its own. It is a mistake to claim human beings are capable of attaining complete objectivity, a so-called God's-eye view, and equally wrong to claim there is no possibility of objective, and therefore scientific, knowledge.

Kant responded to this tension with a synthesis of reason and experience. Knowledge certainly comes to us through sense experience, but the mind actively organizes experience by means of a priori categories or concepts that are presupposed by experience. Kant argued for the categories on the basis of the unity of self-conscious experience, the immediate awareness that thoughts and perceptions occurring simultaneously are mine. For example, my awareness of pain in the foot and the awareness that the pain is mine are "of a piece." The unity of this self-conscious experience could never be drawn from experience alone. This unity that I grasp in my point of view presupposes experience.[5] The a priori categories do not have direct correspondence to independent reality. They have no ontological or metaphysical significance, functioning only as mental structures (unlike Plato's Ideas—which are themselves the structures of reality—and against Descartes, for whom there was correspondence between our innate ideas and external reality).

In Kantian thought, knowledge comes through the synthesis of concepts and experience. Understanding is structured by means of the innate a priori categories and by the imposition of spatial and temporal form onto whatever we perceive. The innate categories apply only to the objects of possible experience (phenomena) and not to objects knowable only to thought (noumena). There is a good bit of confusion about Kant's use of these terms, phenomena and noumena, but since we are interested in understanding Jung's epistemological premises, we can circumvent the scholarly arguments and concentrate on the interpretation that Jung accepted.[6]

The phenomenal world is the world of appearances, the world as we experience it. Ultimate or absolute reality is the realm of the noumenal. We can never *know* the noumenal but only hypothesize its existence on the basis of perception. By virtue of the a priori categories of understanding, the mind organizes reality so that knowledge is possible. Our only referent to noumenal reality is the mental construct; Kant insisted that noumenal is a term useful only to mark the limits of knowledge. We cannot say anything about the noumenal aspect of reality except that it is beyond our capacity to know. Since "God" is a noumenal aspect of human experience, metaphysical arguments about God go beyond the limits of human reason and necessarily lead to contradiction and false claims. It is simply impossible for the human mind to reach beyond the limits of the phenomenal world. And yet, we cannot help but try to do just that.

Human beings naturally seek the "God's-eye" view simply because we are aware that each of us has a particular point of view. Practical reason allows us to figure out what to do, and inference allows us to comprehend the consequences of judgments, but "pure reason" leads us astray, since it attempts to reach a viewpoint that is free of perspective. It is the quest of pure reason that leads us to develop ideas of immortality, freedom, and God. It seems that Kant was able to avoid the solipsism he thought inherent to other philosophies. But in so doing he created a "gap" between mind and world, noumenal and phenomenal.[7] Some have said this gap was so wide that Kant "lost the self."[8] Here, another German philosopher, Friedrich Schleiermacher, plays a part in Jung's epistemology, albeit not so obvious a role as Kant's.

Friedrich Schleiermacher (1768–1883) was a German Protestant philosopher and theologian in the Pietist tradition. Jung mentions him in a 1953 letter, stating that Schleiermacher baptized his grandfather and that "the vast, esoteric, and individual spirit of Schleiermacher was part of the intellectual atmosphere of my father's family. I never studied him, but unconsciously he was for me a *spiritus rector*."[9] In spite of Jung's having called Schleiermacher a "spiritual ancestor," "moving spirit" or unconscious source of inspiration, virtually no attention has been given to the ways in which Jung's ideas appear to reflect Schleiermacher's thought.[10] Since Kant's epistemology was central to Jung's, and Schleiermacher attempted to fix a major problem in Kant's thought (the gap between the noumenal and phenomenal, between the "I" and the "I think"), we need to touch on what Schleiermacher has to say about this.

## Bridging Phenomenal and Noumenal Realities

Schleiermacher, like Jung, was fascinated by Kant's philosophy. This was not, however, an enamored fascination but rather a critical response to what Schleiermacher perceived as dangerous in it. Kant began with reason, moved to the idea of a necessary connection between happiness and virtue, and then postulated "God" as the only way by which the connection could be made. Schleiermacher contrasted this to Christianity, the teachings of which he said begin with God, and reason from the idea of God's will to ideas of virtue.[11] For Schleiermacher, the human mind can never be given the privilege which Kant bestowed on it as "giver of law" to nature. God, not humanity, is the giver of all: "Demonstration presupposes acknowledgment of something else, but cognition of God is the original cognition that underlies all other cognition."[12] The idea of God and its referent must not be confused. Schleiermacher believed that Kant had made just this mistake, and so he sought to identify something within human nature that could maintain the distinction between the "ungiven" God *in se* and the idea of God.[13]

Regarding the role of sense experience in knowing, Schleiermacher spoke of an "organic function" through which we experience our selves and the world. We are *not* fully determined by sense experience, but experience is vital to any kind of knowing—philosophical, religious, or otherwise: "We cannot think except under the form of being. . . . Knowing is the congruence of thinking with being as what is thought."[14] He thought Kant had failed to acknowledge the underlying unity that forms the basis of all experience, in spite of Kantian claims about the unity of self-conscious awareness. Kant, he said, had overlooked the fact that we are embodied; in Kant's thought there was nothing to link the a priori categories of understanding and the external world of objects. *Being* must necessarily be linked to *thinking*; otherwise, it becomes impossible to determine how it is that we are aware of our connection to the world.[15]

Schleiermacher agreed with Kant's attempt to establish theology without grounding it in empirical knowledge, but in making the ethical subject the link between reason, the will, and action, Kant extended the gap between understanding's a priori principles and the objects to which they apply. There was no connection between the "I think" and the pure "I," between the physical self and the thinking self. Kant had tried to solve this through the theory of the all-encompassing "ether" and the idea that the thinking subject must hypothesize itself. Unfortunately, Kant ended up creating a perpetual circle in which the self signifies that which the concept of thought entails. He said the ether is the totality of all possible experience that provides the material for thought. The self is both that which is aware and that *of* which it is aware.[16] Kant's self ends up sounding a great deal like his ether.

Schleiermacher's goal was to break out of this circular argument and understand the body's role in linking us to God. To do this, he had to find a way to affirm "being" without reducing it to "thought." The key to the problem involved his seeing that the Kantian circle expresses only mutual dependence between being and thought. To solve the problem, Schleiermacher rejected intellectual intuitions of Kant's sort and argued in favor of that which the intellect cannot grasp: feeling. Feeling, he said, is not a sensation. It is "subject-less awareness," the unity or oneness of being, or unmediated and immediate self-consciousness. His argument is extremely complex and was worked out over a period of years in lectures, so our discussion here can be only a sketchy outline.

Consciousness is made up of sense impressions that express the capacity to be affected by the external world. Concepts, for Schleiermacher, are not innate to reason. Concepts come about due to reason's expression of the "will to know." Reason is the interior ground of consciousness, or the receiving agent of sense impressions; this means that reason and sensing are co-determinate. The original state of consciousness is a confused unfixed wash of sense impressions. Through a process of contrasting consciousness of things with consciousness of self, of the "I" to "things," determinate consciousness comes into being. Objective and subjective, then, are perceived as a unity accomplished through contrast.

The relation between subject and object is one of "twofold contrast." The world is both determined by and determinate of the subject. If the subject is described as active, the world necessarily will appear as passive, and vice versa. Schleiermacher extends this two-fold contrast to describe the unity of the self as physical and ethical. The activity of reason is both ethical and physical. The unity of the subject rests in a polar relation of active and passive, but what is the link between the "will to think" (passive) and "thought" (active)? Kant's solution to the problem, the unity of self-conscious experience, becomes the point of transition for Schleiermacher.

For Schleiermacher, the capacity to conjecture, to fix things in consciousness, is the pure "I." The modality of positing makes reason possible. This capacity is the self that both thinks and continues to "be" when thought ceases.

All actual thought is dependent on the contrasting relationship between the "will to know" and the "becoming of knowing." Our capacity for thought minus determinate thinking is the "nullpoint" (*Nullpunkt*) or "point of indifference" (*Indifferenzpunkt*), that which is left over when we are not actually thinking. If, as Kant said, the self is determined by thought or reason, then the self would cease to "be" in this nullpoint. Thus, the gap has been delineated.

The nullpoint is the border between the having-just-ceased of one thought and the not-yet-having-begun of another. The pure "I" is the agency that makes thought possible; it is not the thought itself. The self, then, might be thought of as pure potentiality. The nullpoint is the transition between two moments of consciousness, where one thought ends and another has not yet begun. Life can be thought of as a series of transitions from thinking to willing and vice versa, and the self can be thought of as the means of transition between the two functions of thought.

In identifying the border between thinking and willing, Schleiermacher was able to link "thinking" and "being." He took Kant's "unity of self-consciousness" and transformed it from the actual act of combining sense impressions to the *transition point* that makes the combining possible at all. Cognitive thought and organic being are co-determinate but are not the same thing. We must, according to Schleiermacher, assume correspondence between our thoughts and the sense world; we cannot actually know this but must assume it. This presupposition of the unity between thinking and being is the transcendental ground of knowledge. The problem then becomes one of showing how we are aware of this unity.

At the nullpoint, which for Schleiermacher is the gap left between Kant's phenomenal and noumenal realities, thinking both reaches its limit and is the limit. This is object-less awareness, objective consciousness empty of thought. Schleiermacher called this awareness *Anschauung*, immediate unmediated intuition. It is not thinking but rather that which makes thinking possible. At the nullpoint we are conscious of nothing. "Self consciousness viewed apart from all determined content is nothing other than consciousness of the oneness and the belonging together of the two functions,"[17] thinking and being. This is an immediate state of mind, a transcendental standpoint unknowable by means of concepts or judgments. It is an embodied, experiential, empirical encounter of unmediated awareness.

The subjective complement to object-less awareness is subject-less awareness or *Gefühl*. This term has usually been translated as "feeling," but this is somewhat misleading, so I will leave the German term untranslated. It is not sensation, which has to do with the organic, determinate "I." *Gefühl* is the immediate unmediated self-consciousness, the experience of unity or oneness of our own being. It is the point of transition between and within each moment of determinate consciousness. Intuition, then, is the awareness of the null-point from the standpoint of objective consciousness, while feeling is the awareness that "I = I from one moment of consciousness to the next."[18] At the nullpoint, the self is undetermined, unbounded, unlimited, and indistinguishable from all of life. Objectively, it is empty or null with regard to content. Subjectively, it is full; the self is conscious of the self.

Our consciousness of the nullpoint is *felt* or experienced in the identity of physical and ethical—we do not think or will the rupture into consciousness; we feel it. This feeling is intuition's disposition. In this place where thought and action are canceled, or perhaps "on hold," we "simply are the feeling of our nonindividuated self as a part of the natural world. For Schleiermacher, this unbounded state is 'the birth hour of everything living in religion.'"[19] *Gefühl*, as the unmediated awareness of oneness, links being to thinking. It is the embodiment of self, "the sheer embodied self that is the counterbalance to the [Kantian] 'I think.'"[20] There is no subject or object because it is oneness with the organic world, in contrast to Kant's self that was encased in its own thought. In immediate self-consciousness, the null-point, there is cancellation of "being" as self-determining agency that results in the "feeling of utter dependence." This is the religious element in all of life, in which the transcendental ground, or God, is represented within human consciousness. Religion, said Schleiermacher, is "the consciousness of being absolutely dependent, or which is the same thing, of being in a relation with God."[21] God, or the Transcendent, is not experienced in or by the self: God is encountered in unmediated *representation*, as our "immediate feeling of life."[22]

"The feeling of absolute dependence, accordingly, is not to be explained as an awareness of the world's existence, but only as an awareness of the existence of God, as the absolute undivided unity."[23] In other words, at the preconscious level we sense the gap between the end of one thought and the beginning of the next. We feel the rupture of consciousness and at the same time sense that we have not fallen through the gap into fragmentation. We are aware that *something* holds us up, maintains the self as a unity across the gap. This *something, the Absolute*, is God, that upon which we have the awareness of the feeling of utter dependence. The first phase of this feeling is a precognitive, pre-sensate awareness. The second is an actual moment of consciousness which is the religious element; our own self-consciousness is expressed in the consciousness of God. This is not a mystical merging of self with God. Although the nullpoint does refer to that which is absolute, it does not provide knowledge of God *in se*. Schleiermacher is in agreement with Kant here—we can have no knowledge of God *in se*. The experience refers to the self at one with the world and with life itself.[24]

"Religion is to seek this and find it in all that lives and moves, in all growth and change, in all doing and suffering. It is to have life and to know life in immediate feeling, only as such an existence in the Infinite and Eternal. . . . true religion is sense and taste for the Infinite."[25] Schleiermacher said, "The religious self-consciousness . . . leads necessarily in its development to fellowship or communion."[26] There is a "dynamic unity-in-diversity which constitutes the world, wherein individual and community, the organic and the inorganic, the universal and the particular are bound to each other in creative tension . . . each takes on its identity through relation to the other."[27] Everything that exists is grounded in the always-already-there relation to God. Reality is experienced as apparent polarities that are in actuality manifestations of the preexistent "unity-in-diversity" that is the nature of reality. These polarities do not need to be taken up into a greater unity—all that exists is always already grounded in the unity of the Absolute. We are aware of the Absolute in and through the nullpoint and the experience of "utter dependence." This dependence is, as Paul Tillich said, teleological. It has a "moral character, which includes freedom and excludes a pantheistic and deterministic interpretation of the experience of the unconditional."[28]

Theology, for Schleiermacher, is experiential: appeals to authority alone do not suffice. Experience and reality cannot be separated. God is given *in* experience, not derived from it. This theme echoes throughout his elucidation of the doctrine of incarnation:

> As certainly as Christ was a man, there must reside in human nature the possibility of taking up the divine into itself, just as did happen in Christ . . . even if only the *possibility* of this resides in human nature, so that the actual implanting therein of the divine element must be purely a divine and therefore eternal act, nevertheless the temporal appearance of this act in one particular Person must at the same time be regarded as an action of human nature.[29]

Schleiermacher developed an evolutionary view of the incarnation. He said the human nature in Christ has been eternally "coming to be" within the process of the world,[30] and the incarnation itself was a manifestation of "God-consciousness" that is present in all humanity. Although all humans have this consciousness, only Jesus had such a strong and pure God-consciousness that it actually *was* the presence of God in him. In Jesus the God-consciousness was a "perfect indwelling." In us it manifests as the "sense and taste for the infinite," or prereflective awareness of being "absolutely dependent" for our very being on God. Schleiermacher believed this human awareness has the potential to evolve to greater and greater levels of knowing God. Christ differed from us in degree, not in kind, and the difference in degree was in "the constant potency of [Jesus'] God-consciousness, which was a veritable existence of God in Him."[31]

Having surveyed the essentials of Kant's and Schleiermacher's episte-
mologies we are now better situated to understand Jung's claims about the
psychology of human religious experience.

## JUNG'S EPISTEMOLOGY AND RELIGIOUS EXPERIENCE

Kant's influence is obvious in Jung's adoption of the phenomenal/noumenal
distinction regarding the limits of human knowing. Jung wrote explicitly of
Kant's formative influence, and so it is not surprising that some of the criticism of Jung's work involves problems that are inherent in Kant's system.[32]
Although he did acknowledge a connection to Schleiermacher, Jung was not
clear about ways that he had been his "spiritual ancestor." As we delve more
deeply into Jung's psychology of religious experience, however, we see hints
of Schleiermacher's thought throughout. If we accept that Schleiermacher's
interpretation of religion as *Gefühl* (the unmediated awareness of oneness
with and dependence upon that which maintains the self as a unity across the
gap between the end of one thought and another) closes the gap left by Kant
in his explication of the limits of human knowing, Jung's psychology of religion stands on firmer ground.

Paul Bishop analyzed an early poem recently found in the archives of the
Jung Institute in Zurich for what it can tell us of Jung's early religious beliefs,
and it shows hints of Schleiermacher's influence. The poem conveys, among
other themes, the idea that "emotional experience, not mere intellectual adherence to a particular creed, forms the basis of religious conviction. . . .
knowledge must be replaced by some deeper intuition." Bishop concludes
that Jung's early religiousness was a form of nature mysticism—encounter
with the divine in and through the natural world.[33] In this we have perhaps the
first indication that Schleiermacher's thought may have operated implicitly
throughout Jung's exploration of religious experience.

Epistemologically for Jung, the "knowing subject is part of a wider knowledge pool with which the individual is in interaction."[34] Recall that he believed individual mental experience occurs at the conscious, personal unconscious, and collective unconscious levels. Consciousness is an adaptive
accomplishment, and the unconscious is the source of psychological instinctual forces called archetypes, which are the forms or categories that regulate
the instincts.[35] Bear in mind that archetypes are patterns of instinctual behavior arising from the collective unconscious, which is a repository of the universal "ancestral heritage of possibilities of representation" containing the "whole
spiritual heritage of [hu]mankind's evolution, born anew in the brain structure
of every individual" that account for the common themes in humanity's

dreams, myths, and legends.[36] These primordial images are not part of our phenomenal experience; as noumena they can only be intuited psychologically.

Belief is not knowledge for Jung. Religious realities do have a transpersonal basis, arising as they do from the collective unconscious, but because they are filtered through subjective experience they can never be absolutes. Again, the most we can say about God from the psychological standpoint is that "an archetypal image of the Deity" exists.[37] The God-image and statements about it are "psychic processes which are different from their transcendent object."[38]

Now that we are aware of Jung's familiarity with Schleiermacher, some of Jung's comments about the archetypes take on a new dimension. In the previous chapter we discussed the Self archetype, representing the unity of a mature psyche, and which Jung sometimes referred to as "the God within."[39] About the archetypes, Jung said that they are "the hidden foundations of the conscious mind . . . the roots which the psyche has sunk not only in the earth in the narrower sense but in the world in general."[40] Later he said the archetypes function as "the bridge to matter in general."[41] The archetypes function very much in the way that Schleiermacher's nullpoint does to bridge the gap between thinker and thought, matter and spirit, and phenomenal and noumenal. For Schleiermacher, it is at the nullpoint that thought and action are canceled and "consciousness of being absolutely dependent . . . of being in a relation with God" arises.[42] In an interview Jung was once asked whether he believed in God. His response was, "Difficult to answer. I *know*. I don't need to believe. I know."[43] This certainty resonates with the realization of *Gefühl*. Since for Jung it is the encounter with archetypal images and themes in dreams, myths, and religions that forms the basis for the awareness of God, perhaps it is in the experience of *Gefühl* that he found inspiration for his concept of the mature, individuated psyche as "the God within."

Another point of consonance between these two great minds is found in their locating the human encounter with God in the depths of the psyche. Commenting on the conception of God as completely transcendent or "wholly other," Jung wrote that it is "psychologically quite unthinkable for God to be simply the 'wholly other' for a 'wholly other' could never be one of the soul's deepest and closest intimacies—which is precisely what God is."[44] We encounter God in the depths of consciousness as an archetypal, intimate reality. Schleiermacher's conception of the incarnation in terms of "God consciousness" resonates with this perception, as does his evolutionary interpretation of the incarnation. The divinity-in-humanity eternally unfolds within the process of the world, and the particular incarnation in Jesus was a manifestation of the "God-consciousness" potential within all of us. The concept of an evolutionary aspect to the divinity-in-humanity and our consciousness of God is central to one of Jung's most important and difficult works, the *Answer to Job*. There he elaborates his thesis that "the real history of the world is the progressive incarnation of the deity" and shows why we must accept full responsibility for the way our lives are expressions of the image of God within.[45] Now that the epistemological premises of Jungian thought are clarified we are better prepared to understand the claims Jung made in his accounting for the dark and contradictory nature of Yahweh and the "psychological ethics" implicit in his answer to the dilemma of the biblical Job.[46]

## TRANSFORMATION OF THE WESTERN GOD-IMAGE

Jung interpreted the myth of Job as a psychological tale of the unconscious and amoral Western God-image coming to consciousness through its encounter with the man Job.[47] The Book of Job is canonical for Jews and Christians and has been a source of consolation for many thousands over millennia and so it is understandable that Jung's reading of it has engendered much confusion and criticism even to the present day. The work is difficult not only for its main thesis but also because of the many references to obscure and arcane concepts familiar only to those who have extensively studied mythology, astrology, and alchemy.[48] The challenge for us here as we examine Jung's main thesis in *Answer to Job* is to hold fast to this: Jung insisted his theory says nothing about God and a great deal about the Western psyche and our *images* of God. In the preface to this work, Jung entreated his readers to recall that "the image and the statement are psychic processes which are different from their transcendental object; they do not posit it, they merely point to it."[49]

The story in its present form tells of the trials and tribulations faced by a man of great faith who becomes a pawn in a cosmic bet. Job's problems begin when Yahweh calls an assembly of the "sons of the gods" in heaven. God points out to the assembly that Job is a righteous man of great virtue. The satan[50] responds with the claim that it is easy to be virtuous when you have everything and bets Yahweh that Job will change if he is no longer prosperous. Yahweh allows the satan to test Job's faith by raining down on him all sorts of financial, emotional, and physical suffering. Job's friends offer platitudes aimed at justifying God's apparent cruelty and immorality. But no matter the torment visited upon him with God's permission, Job refuses to believe either that his suffering is somehow merited or that God is not just and deserving of worship.

In Jung's reading of the text, the important point is that the man Job remains steadfast and that, in the end, it is Yahweh who is changed, not Job. The wrath of God is finally poured out not on Job but on his friends who, God says, "have not spoken of me what is right, as my servant Job has" (Job 42:7 New Revised Standard Version). The friends, who offered justifications for God's immoral treatment of Job, are punished by God. Job remained steadfast in faith. He never accepted claims that his suffering was just, and for this he was rewarded by God twice over. Jung interprets this to mean that Job, then, is more moral than his God (image). "Whoever knows God has an effect on him. The failure of the attempt to corrupt Job has changed Yahweh's nature."[51]

Yahweh, the unconscious God-image, is a manifestation of the Self archetype and as such is a paradoxical union of opposites. The result of this encounter between man and Yahweh is a vital step toward resolution of the opposition, or the humanization of the god through incarnation. "From Job it is quite obvious that Yahweh behaves like a man with inferior consciousness and an absolute lack of moral self-reflection. In this respect [the] God-image is more limited than man. Therefore God must incarnate."[52] In this way Jung was able to extend his analysis of the transformation of the Western God-image beyond the Book of Job to include the New Testament. To briefly summarize, he said that the story of Jesus as the incarnation of God symbolizes a positive evolution but one which is incomplete. The tension generated by uniting the opposites in Jesus led later Christians to reject the darkness of the collective Shadow that had been so clearly revealed in Job's encounter with Yahweh. This resulted in an incomplete resolution of the paradoxical God problem. What had nearly become a collective individuation of the archetypal cultural Self became instead a splitting into good versus evil. This manifests in the reification of the satan image into a personified appearance of all the rejected qualities in the Devil.[53]

Historical critical study of Job has led to a discovery that lends support to Jung's psychological reading of the text as a record of the transformation of the Western God-image. Job as we have it today is actually a redacted text, made up of a short and very ancient folk tale in chapters 1–2 and 42:10–17, which was used by later writers to frame a long poem, now chapters 3–42:9. The folk tale was well-known in the ancient Mideast; it appears in Egyptian, Sumerian, and Babylonian literature as well as in the Hebrew Bible. Biblical scholars now date the folk tale to as early as the second millennium BCE and the poem to the sixth century BCE. When read separately—the ancient tale first, followed by the more recent text contained in chapters 3–41 and 42:1–9—the differences are clear and striking.

In the folk tale, Job is an innocent and pious man who has never done anything to merit the punishments that rain down on him. He is so devoted to God that Yahweh recognizes his purity and says "there is no one like him on the earth" (Job 1:8). The satan incites Yahweh to torment Job, who limits the game only by forbidding the satan from killing the righteous man. As re-peated misfortune befalls the family, Job's wife insists that cursing God is the only rational response to this horrendously unjustified turn of events, but Job remains steadfast in his faith. Job's three friends come to console him, yet when they see the magnitude of his suffering, they weep, tear their robes, and sit with Job "on the ground seven days and seven nights, and no one spoke a word to him" (Job 2:12–13). Job does not waver in his faith even though he has lost his wealth, property, family, and health. He is so righteous, in fact, that in the midst of his own suffering, he prays not for himself but for his friends! Yahweh responds by restoring Job's fortune twice over, "and Job died, an old man, and full of days" (Job 42:17).

The second story begins with Job cursing the day he was born. He laments his losses, expresses anger at the injustice of it all, and demands that Yahweh show him what he has done to deserve all this suffering. God is silent until the very end, but Job's three friends are quite vocal, offering all sorts of ar-guments in defense of God's justice and goodness. In what may well be the earliest theodicy (defense of the goodness of an omnipotent, benevolent, and just deity in the face of evil and suffering) the writer of this poem offers plat-itudes and arguments that lay the blame not on God but rather on Job—clearly God is just, so Job must deserve all of this! This goes on until chapter 38, when God suddenly speaks "out of the whirlwind" (Job 38:1) to castigate Job: "Where were you when I laid the foundations of the earth?" (Job 38:4). The divine tirade ends when Job declares that he does not understand the awe-someness of God and repents of his failure to see the depths of God's won-der. The Lord punishes Job's *friends* for having attempted to defend Yahweh in spite of the injustice of it all! The poem then ends as "the Lord accepted Job's prayer" on behalf of his friends (Job 42:9).

In the earliest version of Job's experience, Job exhibits an unquestioning and almost childlike acceptance of the torments inflicted upon him without justification. In much the same way that an abused child clings to the belief that her abusive parent has only love for her, Job tells his wife that he must accept the horrors along with the good that had been his lot up to this time. One dare not question; that's just the way of life. In the end, Job, like an abused child who suffers in silence and is rewarded with toys and profession of love, is rewarded two-fold by Yahweh. If Jung is right about the biblical record telling of the progressive maturation of Western humanity's image of God, one would expect the more recent poetic portion of Job to reflect a dif-ferent, more mature and self-assured response to divine capriciousness, and this is precisely what we see.

In the more recent telling of Job's affliction, he no longer sits obedient and silent, accepting without question whatever the erratic and immoral Yahweh allows. Job refuses to accept his friends' platitudes and justifications for God's actions. He now challenges God directly. Instead of Job's being put to the test, we now have Job putting God on trial. Job refuses to accept that the behavior of his unconscious and projected God-image is justifiable. He will no longer sit in silent suffering; he demands an accounting from God. This comparison of the earlier and later versions can be read archetypally as a record of the gradual movement toward consciousness of our responsibility in relation to our conceptions of God.

The ancient folk tale of naive unquestioning acceptance of whatever befalls him is in stark contrast to the audacious challenge offered by the later poetic version of Job's experience. The rewards heaped upon him and the punishments rained down on his friends are quite confusing until we read the text through Jung's lens. Our God-images wreak havoc in the world, causing senseless suffering unless and until we achieve a more balanced and integrated ego consciousness. The writer(s) of the poem were, in this interpretation, closer to individuation and so were able to accept that the God-image is not God *in se*, and also that we must be unflinchingly honest in our relating to the God-images we construct. We humans must accept responsibility for our actions and challenge all acts undertaken in the name of our gods. This insight was apparently too uncomfortable for the later redactors of the biblical text, who used the "cut and paste" method of framing Job's shocking and successful challenge of Yahweh with the more comfortable, unconscious, and less daunting tale of the "patience of Job."

Other scholars have noted trends in the biblical record which tie into Jung's thesis that the scriptures portray an evolving God-image. Two merit mention here: biblical scholar Richard Elliott Friedman and Jack Miles. Miles's book *God: A Biography* was awarded the Pulitzer Prize. In it he analyzed the scriptures from a literary point of view to trace character development in its portrayal of God. His conclusion is the same as Jung's: God required engagement with humanity in order to discern His own thoughts and intentions, and once this is done, God moves into the background of the biblical story.[54] Coincidentally, Friedman's book was published the same year and offered a compatible analysis done from the standpoint of biblical, not literary, scholarship. In *The Disappearance of God: A Divine Mystery* (later republished as *The Hidden Face of God*) Friedman traces the gradual disappearance of God as an active figure in the scriptures and seeks the meaning of this phenomenon, which he sets alongside the appearance in the nineteenth and twentieth centuries of philosophical and theological rhetoric about the "death of God" and the mystical Jewish concept of *tikkun*, restoration.[55] Friedman's is a theological interpretation of the evolving divine-human relationship and so differs to some degree from Jung's psychological one, but taken together, these construals are quite powerful.

When read chronologically, the Hebrew Bible begins with God as an active and visible presence which, over the course of time, gradually recedes from public view. In the earliest books, God is intimately involved in creation; in Genesis, God walks in the Garden, talks with human beings, and even engages in physical combat with Jacob in the form of an angel. After Moses, no one sees God directly anymore, who begins to speak only through prophets. God's fading away continues until finally, in the book of Esther, God is not even mentioned. Concomitantly, we see increased human participation in and confrontation of divine actions: Adam disobeys God, Abraham questions God's decisions, and Jacob fights with God (as an angel) and when he survives is given the name Israel, which means something like "wrestles with God." In the Hebrew Bible, miracles are done by God at first and then are performed through humans, until finally they also fade away. Likewise human rulers gradually displace God. David rules as God's anointed, and by the end of the chronological reading, human beings who do not even worship God, the Persians, are in control.

As God's presence fades, humanity's responsibility increases. All of this is especially intriguing given that this movement away from divine micromanagement toward human responsibility happens as we read according to the internal chronology of the Bible. Since these texts were written over many centuries and when gathered together into the canon were not placed according to chronology of writing dates, this phenomenon could not be something that was consciously written into the individual texts. There is a chronological evolution in the God-image that does not become apparent until one places the texts in that order.

Friedman traces the progressive divine hiddenness beyond the end of the Hebrew Bible into the period of Second Temple Judaism and early Christianity. Human responsibility and authority jump dramatically in the inter-testamental period in two ways: with the development of authority vested in the Oral Torah (rabbinic interpretation of the scriptures) and in the ultimate step of God coming-to-be in human form.

Although Friedman's examination of the "death of God" phenomenon and consonance between Big Bang cosmology and mystical Judaism's teachings are fascinating, we need not examine them here in order to understand his point. The mystical Jewish concept of *tikkun* has to do with the idea that creation came into being when a cosmic catastrophe resulted in the "shattering of the vessels."[56] As a result, something of the divine remains in all aspects of creation. Although the major portion of restoration of the cosmos is accomplished by God, the completion of it depends on humanity. Humanity is charged with the responsibility of restoring the world to its spiritual place through observance of Torah and contemplative activity:[57]

At opposite poles, both [humanity] and God encompass with their being the entire cosmos. However, whereas God contains all . . . [humanity's] role is to complete this process by being the agent through whom all the powers of creation
are fully activated and made manifest . . . the process of creation involves the
departure of all from the One and its return to the one, and the crucial turning
point in this cycle takes place within [humanity] at the moment [we begin] to
develop an awareness of [our] own true essence.[58]

What this means, in Jung's words, is that "the real history of the world seems
to be the progressive incarnation of the deity."[59] We must become participants
in the Transcendent Reality, in the Divine Nature, because we play a vital role
in the unfolding of creation.[60]

Humanity must accept a new responsibility in relation to God. Through our
conscious participation in the continuing incarnation of the noumenal Transcendent Reality into the phenomenal world of experience we become adults,
responsible for our own existence. This responsibility entails the realization
that not only do we depend upon God but also God depends upon us.[61] "Individuation and individual existence are indispensable for the transformation
of God. Human consciousness is the only seeing eye of the Deity."[62]

Jung was deeply disturbed by the proliferation of technologies of mass destruction. He insisted that "everything now depends on man: immense power
of destruction is given into his hand, and the question is whether he can resist
the will to use it, and can temper his will with the spirit of love and wisdom."[63]
The symbols that rise up from the unconscious are opposites; our God-images
call us to be just, loving, and merciful, and they also often demand of us horrendous acts of violence. We must both worship and fear our gods. The God-
image "fills us with evil as well as with good . . . and because he wants to become man, the uniting of [God's] antinomy must take place in [us]."[64]

In this psychological ethic, humanity must assist God by becoming conscious. "The importance of consciousness is so great that one cannot help sus-
pecting the element of *meaning* to be concealed somewhere within all the
monstrous, apparently senseless biological turmoil, and that the road to its
manifestation was ultimately found on the level of warm-blooded vertebrates
possessed of a differentiated brain."[65] Using more specifically theological
language, we can say that through the humanization of the God-image, the divine and human natures are united in one comprehensive, perichoretic
process. Redemption is a dialectic process through which the God-image re-
deems us as we redeem our gods.[66] This is the point of Jung's *Answer to Job*:
we human beings must take responsibility for the transformation of our immoral God-images. This can only be accomplished as each of us works toward personal psychological maturity in the context of communal evolution.

## NOTES

1. Psychological interpretations based on Jungian premises have often been criticized because the enthusiasm of some interpreters leads them to elevate Jung to the status of a demigod who came to reveal a new "epoch" in human evolution. This is truly unfortunate. Jung himself recognized the danger and was reluctant to agree to establishment of the Zurich Institute in 1948 because of this risk. Two years before the institute opened, he wrote, "'I can only hope and wish that no one becomes 'Jungian.' . . . I stand for no doctrine.'" He only agreed to the institute because he hoped that it would become a center for serious research into the psychology of religious experience, mythologies, and dreams, not a center dedicated to elaboration of the more esoteric aspects of his writings. Intent on ensuring that his work not be treated as dogma or texts for the founding of a system of psychology-as-theology, he wrote that "analytical psychology only helps us to find the way to the religious experience that makes us whole. It is not this experience itself, nor does it bring it about." C. G. Jung, *Letters, 1951–1961*, trans. R. F. C. Hull, ed. Gerhard Adler and Aniela Jaffé (London: Routledge & Kegan Paul, 1975), 265.

2. Jung, *Letters, 1951–1961*, 518–19.

3. C. G. Jung, *Letters, 1906–1950*, trans. R. F. C. Hull, ed. Gerhard Adler and Aniela Jaffé (London: Routledge & Kegan Paul, 1973), 375.

4. Roger Scruton, *Kant: A Very Short Introduction* (Oxford: Oxford University Press, 2001), 16.

5. Scruton, *Kant*, 44. Much of the discussion of Kant's thought follows Scruton's excellent little book.

6. Allen Wood, for example, argues that Kant offered two incompatible interpretations of the phenomenal/noumenal and says that attempts to reconcile them are simply wrong. *Kant. Blackwell "Great Minds" Series*, ed. Steven Nadler (Malden, MA: Blackwell, 2005).

7. Eckhart Förster, "Is There a 'Gap' in Kant's Critical System?" *Journal of the History of Philosophy* 25, no. 4 (October 1987): 533–55.

8. Thandeka, "Schleiermacher's 'Dialektik': The Discovery of the Self That Kant Lost," *Harvard Theological Review* 85, no. 4 (October 1992): 433–52.

9. C. G. Jung, *Letters*, trans. R. F. C. Hull, ed. Gerhard Adler and Aniela Jaffé, Bollingen Series 95:2 (Princeton, NJ: Princeton University Press, 1973), 115.

10. Marilyn Nagy, *Philosophical Issues in the Psychology of C. G. Jung* (Albany, NY: SUNY Press, 1991), quotes Jung in part on this but does not explore the issue beyond its significance as a biographical note. Paul Bishop, in his essay "C. G. Jung and 'Naturmystik': The Early Poem 'Gedanken in Einer Frühlingsnacht,'" *German Life and Letters* 56, no. 4 (October 2003): 327–43, notes the importance of feeling, or "Gefühl," for several of Jung's predecessors, and mentions Schleiermacher among them. More will be said about this.

11. Richard Crouter, "Introduction," in *On Religion: Speeches to Its Cultured Despisers*, by Friedrich Schleiermacher, trans. Richard Crouter (Cambridge: Cambridge University Press, 1988), 20–24.

12. Friedrich Schleiermacher, *Dialectic, or the Art of Doing Philosophy: A Study of the 1811 Notes*, trans. Terrence N. Tice (Atlanta: Scholar's Press, 1996), 29.

13. Thandeka, *The Embodied Self: Friedrich Schleiermacher's Solution to Kant's Problem of the Empirical Self* (Albany, NY: SUNY Press, 1995), 22. Much of the following discussion is based on this fascinating work, as well as her earlier "Schleiermacher's 'Dialektik'" cited above.

14. Schleiermacher, *Dialectic*, 15n25, 16–17.

15. Thandeka, *Embodied Self*, 3.

16. Thandeka, *Embodied Self*, 23–29.

17. Schleiermacher, quoted in Thandeka, *Embodied Self*, 92.

18. Thandeka, *Embodied Self*, 95.

19. Thandeka, *Embodied Self*, 96.

20. Thandeka, *Embodied Self*, 99.

21. Friedrich Schleiermacher, *The Christian Faith*, ed. H. R. MacIntosh and J. S. Stewart (Edinburgh: T & T Clark, 1989), 12.

22. Thandeka, *Embodied Self*, 102.

23. Schleiermacher, *Christian Faith*, 132.

24. Thandeka, "Schleiermacher's 'Dialektik,'" 451–52.

25. Friedrich Schleiermacher, *On Religion: Speeches to its Cultured Despisers*, trans. John Oman (Louisville, KY: Westminster John Knox Press, 1994), 36–39.

26. Schleiermacher, *Christian Faith*, 26.

27. Schleiermacher, *Christian Faith*, 40.

28. Paul Tillich said Schleiermacher's feeling of utter dependence "was rather near to what is called in the present system 'ultimate concern about the ground and meaning of our being.'" *Systematic Theology*, vol. 1 (Chicago: University of Chicago Press, 1951), 42.

29. Schleiermacher, *Christian Faith*, §13.

30. Schleiermacher, *Christian Faith*, §97.

31. Schleiermacher, *Christian Faith*, §94.

32. For criticisms of Jung's epistemology and methods see Nagy, *Philosophical Issues*; Michael Palmer, *Freud and Jung on Religion* (London: Routledge, 1997); among others.

33. Paul Bishop, "C. G. Jung and 'Naturmystik,'" 327–43.

34. Renos K. Papadopoulos, "Jung's Epistemology and Methodology," in *The Handbook of Jungian Psychology: Theory, Practice, and Applications*, ed. Renos K. Papadopoulos (London: Routledge, 2006), 41.

35. C. G. Jung, *The Structure and Dynamics of the Psyche*, in *The Collected Works*, trans. R. F. C. Hull, ed. H. Read, M. Fordham, G. Adler, and W. McGuire, vol. 8, Bollingen Series (Princeton, NJ: Princeton University Press, 1953–1983), paras. 283–342.

36. C. G. Jung, *The Archetypes and the Collective Unconscious*, in *The Collected Works*, trans. R. F. C. Hull, ed. H. Read, M. Fordham, G. Adler, and W. McGuire, vol. 9/1, Bollingen Series 20 (Princeton, NJ: Princeton University Press, 1968/1980), paras. 87–110.

37. C. G. Jung, *Psychology and Religion: The Terry Lectures* (New Haven, CT: Yale University Press, 1938/1966), 73.

38. C. G. Jung, *Answer to Job*. In *The Portable Jung*, ed. Joseph Campbell (New York: Penguin Press, 1952/1976), para. 558.

39. C. G. Jung, *Aion: Researches into the Phenomenology of the Self*, trans. R. F. C. Hull, ed. H. Read, M. Fordham, G Adler, and W. McGuire, vol. 9/2, Bollingen Series 20 (Princeton, NJ: Princeton University Press, 1959/1969), 34, 63, 109.

40. C. G. Jung, "Mind and Earth," in *The Collected Works*, trans. R. F. C. Hull, ed. H. Read, M. Fordham, G. Adler, and W. McGuire, vol. 10, Bollingen Series (Princeton, NJ: Princeton University Press, 1927/1931), para. 53.

41. C. G. Jung, "On the Nature of the Psyche," in *The Collected Works*, trans. R. F. C. Hull, ed. H. Read, M. Fordham, G. Adler, and W. McGuire, vol. 8, Bollingen Series (Princeton, NJ: Princeton University Press, 1947/1954), para 420.

42. Schleiermacher, *Christian Faith*, 12.

43. C. G. Jung, *C. G. Jung Speaking: Interviews and Encounters*, ed. William McGuire and R. F. C. Hull, Bollingen Series 97 (Princeton, NJ: Princeton University Press, 1977), 428.

44. C. G. Jung, *Psychology and Alchemy*, in *The Collected Works*, trans. R. F. C. Hull, ed. H. Read, M. Fordham, G. Adler, and W. McGuire, vol. 12, Bollingen Series (Princeton, NJ: Princeton University Press, 1980), para. 11n6.

45. Jung, *Letters, 1951–1961*, 435–36.

46. Edward F. Edinger, *The New God-Image: A Study of Jung's Key Letters Concerning the Evolution of the Western God-Image*, ed. Diane D. Cordic and Charles Yates (Wilmette, IL: Chiron Publications, 1996).

47. Some of the ideas contained in this section were first published in my "A Jungian Perspective on Religious Violence and Personal Responsibility," *CrossCurrents* 56 (Spring 2006): 16–24.

48. For readers interested in reading *Answer to Job* for themselves, Paul Bishop has published an excellent companion guide: *Jung's Answer to Job: A Commentary* (New York: Brunner-Routledge, 2002).

49. Jung, *Answer to Job*, 526.

50. At the time the Book of Job was written, Satan had not yet become a personified individual manifestation of evil. The Hebrew word translated as "Satan" in modern English translations comes from a root term meaning "obstacle." The satan was originally a divine servant who acted as a kind of prosecuting attorney who was humanity's, not God's, adversary.

51. Jung, *Answer to Job*, 556.

52. Jung, *Letters*, 1622.

53. Jung said the Christian doctrine of the Trinity shows an imbalance in the divine nature, but he was not always clear on the missing element. Sometimes he focused on the absence of darkness as manifested in the split of Christ and Satan, and sometimes the lack of a feminine aspect. He saw the Roman Catholic elevation of Mary by the 1950 papal proclamation of her bodily assumption into heaven as a hopeful sign of movement toward more balance in the Western God-image.

54. Jack Miles, *God: A Biography* (New York: Knopf, 1995).

55. Richard Elliott Friedman, *The Disappearance of God: A Divine Mystery* (Boston: Little, Brown, 1995).

56. Friedman, *Disappearance of God*, 230.

57. Gershom Scholem, *Kabbalah* (New York: Dorset Press, 1987), 138–44.

58. Scholem, *Kabbalah*, 152.

59. Jung, *Letters*, 435–36; quoted in Edinger, *New God-Image*, 89.

60. C. G. Jung, *Memories, Dreams, Reflections*, trans. Richard and Clara Winston, ed. Aniela Jaffé (New York: Vintage Books, 1961/1989), 256.

61. Jung, quoted in Edinger, *New God-Image*, 87.

62. Jung, quoted in Edinger, *New God-Image*, 75.

63. Jung, *Answer to Job*, 636.

64. Jung, *Answer to Job*, 638.

65. Jung, *Memories, Dreams, Reflections*, 339.

66. John P. Dourley, "The Religious Significance of Jung's Psychology," *International Journal for the Psychology of Religion* 5, no. 2 (1995): 73–89.

*Chapter Seven*

# Concluding Reflections: We Must Become More Moral Than Our Gods[1]

Violent conflict results from choice—the choices of leaders and people—and is facilitated through the institutions that bind them.[2]

Religion gives us "assurance and strength so that [we] may not be overwhelmed by the monsters of the universe."[3] The human psyche has not evolved as rapidly as have our intellect and technological capabilities, and so in a sense the unconscious has been left behind. Speaking somewhat prophetically about fifty years ago, Jung said that over the previous century, the unconscious has been forced into "a defensive position which expresses itself in a universal will to destruction. The political and social 'isms' of our day preach every conceivable ideal" while "creating a chaos controlled by terrorism" that leads to a kind of "degradation and slavery" of the individual. How are we to deal with these cultural monsters? They cannot be tamed "collectively, because the masses are not changed unless the individual changes. . . . The bettering of a general ill begins with the individual, and then only when he makes himself and not others responsible."[4]

For the truly religious individual, all of life is informed by faith. Religions are meaning-making systems and as such necessarily inform politics and social life. The mechanisms through which religious ideas are transmuted into claims that we must slaughter one another in order to please our gods are, as we have seen, complex and interwoven with all aspects of human life. From the remnants of our evolutionary past that continue to push us toward preference for those most like ourselves, to the most complex cultural and situational factors, there are dynamic at work that, under the proper conditions, result in religious violence. Some of the identified causes are things over which we have very little direct control—the evolutionary process is a prime example. But once we consider the implications of social psychological research

119

and psychoanalytic theories of the relation between our sensitivity to situational factors, the sense of self, and violence, impotence in the face of it all is attenuated. Yes, the problem of religious violence has been with us from the start of religious history. Yes, the causes are complex. And, yes, there is something that we can at least begin to do about it. Violence in the name of our gods will not cease overnight, but perhaps in the course of a generation some real changes in human history may come about if enough of us become cognizant of the dynamics at work.

Religious ideologies are most likely to play a role in conflict when combined with nationalism or political demands for self-determination. All God-images (including any referent to the transcendent, whether conceptualized anthropomorphically or not) are to a great degree manifestations of cultural and evolutionary processes. If a numinous (from the Latin *nuere*, "to show signs") image like the God-concept is believed to actually *be* that to which the image can in actuality only point, potentially dangerous ego inflation ensues. Since the God-image is identical with the archetypal Self, "everything that happens to the God-image has an effect on the latter. Any uncertainty about the God-image causes a profound uneasiness in the self . . . *the destruction of the God-image is followed by the annulment of the human personality*."[5]

On this, archetypal psychology and Terror Management theorists agree. Challenges to our God-images hit us at the core of our being. When this happens to individuals who have not worked to become aware of the forces at work in their own unconscious minds, a most dangerous situation exists, since an inadequately functioning ego-Self dynamic makes one especially susceptible to archetypal contents within the collective unconscious. The individual becomes more and more subject to situational influences, prone to "psychic infection" by collective movements which bolster confidence in the validity of one's idealizations and projections. When religious practitioners and teachings play upon the shame-humiliation dynamic by manipulating interpretation of the idealized object denigration of oneself intensifies. When the idealized object (God, a human leader believed to speak on behalf of God, etc.) is seen as punitive or as desiring vengeance, splitting the world into all good and all bad occurs. This shame-humiliation dynamic is part of the process which leads to projection of unacceptable psychic contents onto others. Projection allows us to maintain the ego inflation born of ego-Self identification. In situations like this, self-righteousness and power seeking operate as defenses against the shame that challenges one's reified sense of self. The end result can be a kind of narcissistic rage wherein the ego has become so inflated and reified that others who do not agree are not seen an others so much as recalcitrant parts of one's own expanded self. The ego, as the center of subjective identity, has become so inflated that it swallows up objective reality. All empathy for the other ceases since, for all intents and purposes, they have become problematic aspects of one's inner reality that must be made to "toe the line."

These dynamics help to explain why collectivistic cultures, as noted in our discussion of James Waller's work on genocide, are more prone to conflict born of in-group/out-group distinctions than individualistic ones. In collectivistic cultures populated by what Jung called the Traditional or Archaic Man, the first step toward ego-Self identification has already been taken by virtue of one's identity being defined in terms of fixed and stable group membership. Membership in groups led by strong charismatic leaders provides a "comfort zone" within which the individual can project the potentially overpowering energy of the God-image onto the leader and the disturbing dark aspects of the Shadow onto outsiders. Since the archetypes are representations of tradition, modernization and secularization are threatening at deeply unconscious levels in such cultures. The member of a collectivist culture is more prone to projection because of the "undifferentiated state of his mind and his consequent inability to criticize himself."[6] Hitler's impact on the German people makes a great deal of sense when viewed from this perspective. His power came not from originality of the message but precisely because he had an uncanny ability to express the contents of the German collective unconscious.

Jung's analysis of Hitler in a 1939 interview is illuminating here. He said that Hitler's power arose from the fact that he was "a megaphone which voice[d] the mood or the psychology of the eighty million German people" and we cannot understand him "apart from a consideration of the unconscious factors. . . . Hitler has sacrificed his individuality . . . to this almost complete subordination to collective unconscious forces. . . . He is virtually the nation. And the trouble about a nation is that it does not keep its word and has no honor. . . . [It] is a blind force."[7] Although he did not use this terminology, Jung is speaking here about what happens when the conceptual entity "nation" becomes reified. The shame-humiliation dynamic was very much at work in the German psyche during the early twentieth century, and Hitler was "the mirror of that inferiority complex" which had become part of the German psyche as a result of the disastrous outcome of World War I and the Treaty of Versailles. Reification of national and ethnic identities, like religions, provides an entity onto which groups can project their collective selves. Hitler, as the voice of the German collective unconscious, articulated the rhetoric of ego inflation and paved the way for ego identification with the new god, the Aryan Race. When religions and national identities are reified the potential for violence is greatly multiplied.

Philip Zimbardo's prison experiment and Stanley Milgram's "shocking" research have shown how powerfully influential situational factors are for the average person. Contrary to our Western idealization of the individual, we have seen that "individual behavior is largely under the control of social forces and environmental contingencies rather than personality traits, character, will power."[8] The group grants validity to the individual only insofar as she accepts its canons. This helps to explain the root cause of the upsurge in violent acts by Muslim jihadists in recent times. Globalization and the myriad other factors explored in this work are part of the problem but perhaps more for noneconomic reasons than critics of globalization have assumed. Viewed through the lens constructed here, globalization plays a role in violence because the challenge it offers is not simply to one's cultural and social world; it calls into question the God-image. Threats to our images of God, particularly when we have succumbed to ego inflation, threaten to bring about dissolution of our very selves.

This is so because the encounter with the God-image happens at the null-point of consciousness wherein all thought and action are cancelled. Our image of God arises from the experience of *Gefühl*, utter dependence upon *something* greater than ourselves that bridges the "space" between the cessation of one thought and the start of another, thereby holding us, in a sense, together where the determinate self ceases to be, and the indeterminate unmediated awareness of numinosity—*existence itself*—is experienced as the unity of being. In this "space" the individual psyche comes into contact with the collective psyche; perhaps the collective unconscious is just this—the unbounded state of nonindividuated selfhood in the "between" of knowing and being. At the nullpoint, the God-image/Self archetype holds us and keeps the ego from the fragmentation that threatens. The challenge of individuation is to become conscious of this without succumbing to the temptation to reify the ego/Self in response to the threat of permanent rupture between knowing and being.

On this point, the teachings of Buddhism have come closest of all the religions in understanding. The Buddha taught that our tendency to reify the self (ego) is the source of all suffering, and his guidelines for living encoded in the Noble Eightfold Path are aimed at this problem. Meditation is central to Buddhist practice because it brings one to the nullpoint, wherein we achieve awareness that the self to which we are so attached is in actuality an illusion. In fact, the quests for Buddhist enlightenment and Jungian individuation are similar enterprises. Individuation, like enlightenment, involves making conscious those forces at work in the unconscious. Recall that in the process of individuation, the persona (social mask) is broken down, allowing the emergence of archetypal material into consciousness, differentiation of ego from archetypes, and gradual integration of these energies through taking conscious nonjudgmental ownership of them. The end result is establishment of the self as a midpoint between the ego (individual) and the collective.

Jung saw parallels between the Christian incarnation as the coming-to-consciousness of the God-image and the Buddhist mythology of enlightenment. In Buddhism, the Doctrine of Interdependent Origination teaches that we are caught in the cycle of rebirth, bound by the twelve links of the chain of unsatisfactoriness (*dukkha*) that characterizes existence. The most important of the links is ignorance of the truth that there is no enduring, unchanging self. Awareness of no-self is central in Buddhism because the illusion that "I" am an unchanging entity leads to actions aimed at protection of the ego. This is the basic human problem, what the Buddha described as grasping after permanence. Once the link of ignorance is broken by a practitioner's becoming conscious of the truth of no-self, it is possible to attain Nirvana. Jung said that the "Buddha's insight and the Incarnation in Christ break the chain [of suffering] through the intervention of the enlightened human consciousness."[9] In the Buddhist experience of no-self, we have resonance with the nullpoint wherein all thought and action are cancelled, the determinate self ceases to be, and the indeterminate unmediated awareness of existence itself is experienced as a unity of being.

Although Jung's system was certainly shaped by his Western worldview, he studied non-Western religious thought and practices extensively and in the process may have hit upon a nearly universal aspect of the human religious pursuit. In the Sufi form of Islam, for example, this life is a journey that proceeds along horizontal and vertical paths. The horizontal journey involves physical birth, life, and death. The vertical journey is one that potentially culminates in *al-fanā*, annihilation or extinction of self, and *al-baqā*, "annihilation of annihilation" or "subsistence in God."[10] On the surface this may sound like a practice aimed at fusion of ego/self with one's image of God, but this is not the case. Islamic scholar Seyyed Hossein Nasr says that Sufism is the message "of the Centre at the periphery" which guides its practitioners "from the phenomena to the noumena, from the form to the meaning." Although all of Islam is about *tawhîd*, the unity or oneness of God, Sufism takes this as the axis of its metaphysics and teaches that, although the world and God are not identical, to the degree that the world is real, it "cannot be completely other than God; were it to be so it would become a totally independent reality . . . and would destroy the absoluteness and the Oneness that belong to God alone."[11] This means that, since God is one, each of us must attain wholeness through the integration of body, mind, and spirit.

Sufi forms of prayer function to eliminate separation from the divine; in particular, *dhikr* (invocation or repetition of the names of God) leads to the integration of the soul as an offering to God. In the words of Ibn al`Arîf, the tenth-century Sufi, "If thou becomest absent from thy heart, He will install Himself there."[12] Nasr says that this is what Islam, as submission to the will

of God, really means. The Sufi turns toward unity first through observance of
life according to *Sharīah*, divine law as revealed in the Quran, and interpreted through the life example and sayings of the Prophet Muhammad,
scholarly consensus, and analogical reasoning. The Prophet is "the prototype
of the human individual and the human collectivity." His lack of education is
symbolic of the extinction (*al-fanā*) of all human aspects before God, and the
Muslim, in living according to the *Sharī`ah*, places her entire existence in
God's hands.[13] This is why peace activist Fethullah Gülen insists that "a real
Muslim, one who understands Islam in every aspect, cannot be a terrorist."[14]
One who truly understands the concept of divine oneness understands that to
harm any aspect of creation is to harm oneself and God.

Similar themes of unitive experience appear in the mystical expressions of
many of the world's major religious traditions. In philosophical Hinduism,
the basic human problem is ignorance of the true nature of reality as one. The
Absolute, or *Brahman*, is present in everything, and the material forms of the
cosmos are illusory manifestations that cause us to believe that we are separate selves. The goal of meditative practice is to achieve comprehension that
all is *Brahman*. Once we see that separateness is illusory, the importance of
*ahimsa* (the intent to do no harm to any living being) becomes clear. This is
the basis upon which Gandhi developed his interpretation of the *Bhagavad
Gita* and which eventuated in his powerful teachings on *satyagraha*, nonviolent creative resistance to oppression.

The ancient philosophical Hindu concept of Yoga Nidra, or Yogic Conscious Sleep, is an intriguing religious teaching that seems targeted similarly
to the individuation process. Meditative techniques are used to allow the practitioner to enter the state of conscious sleep wherein, it is said, the deepest patterns of thought and emotion, called *samskaras*, are found. The state is a kind
of objectless/subjectless awareness during which one is able to observe the
*samskaras* and gradually lessen their intensity. Since negative karma is
thought to accrue primarily as a result of attachment to the self as a separate
entity distinct from the Absolute reality, this practice is very powerful in advancing the student toward *moksha*, release from the cycle of rebirth.

There is a very long tradition of Christian meditation aimed at states of
union with the divine, beginning in the earliest centuries of the faith with the
Desert Fathers and Mothers, men and women who sought God in the solitude
of the deserts of North Africa and the Middle East. In Eastern Christianity, the
*heyschastic* (from the Greek for stillness, quiet) tradition is focused on encounter with God not *in se* but in and through the divine energies. As Gregory
Palamas (1296–1358), a foundational theologian for Orthodox theology, said,
"Since one can participate in God and since the . . . essence of God is absolutely above participation, there exists something between [the essence and

created reality]. . . . Thus He makes Himself present to all things . . . by His creative and providential energies."[15] These themes appear contemporaneously in Western Europe. Meister Eckhart (1260–1327), for example, was a German theologian who taught that "man should be empty of self and all things . . . he should be reconstructed in the simple good that God is."[16]

Teachers of mystical forms of practice appear across the history of the faith, including Hildegard of Bingen (1098–1179), Julian of Norwich (1342–1416), the unknown author of the fourteenth-century English texts *Cloud of Unknowing* and the *Book of Privy Council*, Teresa of Ávila (1515–1582), Brother Lawrence (1610–1691), and the founder of the Quaker denomination, George Fox (1624–1691). In the Quaker tradition, each human being has within the Inner Light of God which enables us to have a direct interior experience of God. Because this experience is both individual and communal, the traditional Quaker worship service involves the community coming together to sit in silent listening. As Rufus Jones (1863–1948) said, this silence can be "an actual moment of mutual and reciprocal correspondence with God. The actual meeting of man with God and God with man is the very crown and culmination of what we can do with our human life here on earth."[17] Significantly, the Quakers have been vocal and active supporters of human rights, justice, and nonviolence.

The idea of mystical union is important in some forms of Judaism as well. In Kabbalistic and Hasidic Judaism, *devekut*, or "communion," results in transformation of the human soul such that it becomes part of the "All" or "enters into God."[18] This concept is linked in Hasidic thought to the task of restoration, *tikkun*, discussed previously. In the mystical creation narrative, a consequence of the "shattering of the vessels" that resulted in the material cosmos is that sparks or fragments of the divine light have been scattered throughout creation. Humanity's task is to work with God through mystical practices and striving for justice in the world in order to "raise the sparks" to their original unity.[19]

Isaac Luria (1534–1572) taught that this concept of creation through the "shattering of the vessels" explains humanity's dual inclination toward both good and evil. He developed spiritual practices aimed at identifying the "root of the soul" and the wounds impinging on it caused by the broken vessels. In Lurianic Judaism, each of us must work to heal our individual souls, through meditative prayer and moral action, in order to repair the cosmos.[20] Humanity and God are partners in this enterprise.

All of these unitive practices are designed to enable the experience of the unmediated awareness of oneness with and dependence upon that which maintains the self as a unity across the gap between the end of one thought and another. In these practices the self is, in Friedrich Schleiermacher's terms, pure potentiality. Through prayer, mediation, and so forth, one achieves a state of objectless and subjectless awareness. This is an embodied, experiential, empirical encounter with unmediated awareness (*Gefühl*) through which the self is known as undetermined unboundedness that is indistinguishable from all of life. This sounds very much like what Heinz Kohut was describing with the concept of cosmic narcissism, wherein the person experiences self-transcendence in a "supraindividual and timeless existence" and is capable of empathy for the cosmos, as a unique form of human psychological integration.

This discussion is not meant to imply that all of these practices are identical—nor do I mean that mystical religious experiences are reducible to the psychological process of individuation. The consonances noted here are striking, but at the same time the differences in interpretation among the various religions must be kept in mind. What this discussion does indicate is that there is a distinctive and universal aspect of human psychology that seems to play a role in certain kinds of religious experience and which also sounds very much like psychoanalytic theories about healthy selves.

A further caution is in order here. The practices we have examined are not to be confused with the spiritual rhetoric of "killing in order to heal," which has been shown to encourage participation in violence, especially when combined with demands for unquestioning obedience to human authorities who claim to speak for God.[21] Spiritual teachings and practices designed to lead the individual to transformative integration through encounter with the numinous can be perverted by charismatic narcissists, and this is why my focus here has been on individual transformation as the vital first step toward collective transformation. It is not insignificant that, in all of the mystical religious traditions, practitioners are admonished to engage the techniques only under the guidance of a more experienced and spiritually developed guide.

The rhetoric of life through death, healing through killing, has been literalized and used by nonindividuated narcissistic people to add fuel to the fires of violence in all of the religions. For example, when Martin Luther (1483–1546) wrote that "when God brings to life, he does it by killing,"[22] he was speaking about a spiritual experience which Christian mystics have understood in terms of union with God. Yet, once his religious teachings became part of the political struggles and formation of national identity of the nascent German nation, Luther and his rhetoric of life through death became powerful supporters of religious warfare.

In 1985 Pope John Paul II (1920–2005; pope from 1978–2005), a strong voice against the 2003 U.S. invasion of Iraq, expressed the impact of mystical encounter with the numinous:

Did not Eckhart teach his disciples: "All that God asks you most pressingly is to go out of yourself—and let God be God in you"? One could think that, in separating himself from creatures, the mystic leaves his brothers, humanity, behind . . . on the contrary, the mystic is marvelously present to them on the only level where he can truly reach them, that is in God.[23]

## CAN WE BECOME MORE MORAL THAN OUR GODS?

The evolution of human cognition is a double-edged sword. It has achieved its current heights in large measure because of the capacity we humans have for pooling our resources through the development of languages and cultures. Recall that cultures are storehouses maintained across generations through symbolic technologies which make it possible for us to work together in organizing social experience and knowledge. The very mechanisms which made this possible are the means through which the potential for us to be influenced by the collective projections of a culture's unacknowledged Shadow arises. For "what else is the collective unconscious but the ingrained emotional patterns and unthought thoughts that fill us with the prejudices we prefer to conceive as choices?"[24]

Archetypal psychology has given rise to a new field of biblical study in recent decades. Walter Wink, one of the pioneers of the psychological reading of the Christian scriptures, gives an excellent illustration of the way archetypal forces influence life in his reading of the New Testament. In an award-winning series of three books, he posits that the New Testament language of "principalities and powers" is a general term that designates the outer and inner manifestations of power in human social life. The inner or spiritual aspect of institutional and national powers was understood symbolically during the first century in terms of angelic and demonic forces. "Power must become incarnate, institutionalized or systemic in order to be effective." This incarnation of power manifests as the "spirit" or *Zeitgeist* of a nation or organization. "What the ancients called 'spirits' or 'angels' or 'demons' were actual entities, only they were not hovering in the air. They were incarnate in . . . skin and bones, or an empire, or its mercenary armies."[25] Religious groups are transformed from life-affirming collectives to destructive manifestations of the demonic when their members remain unconscious of this truth.[26] The first step toward wholeness and life-affirming choices requires that we become conscious of these issues and work to understand when we are acting from conscious choice and when we are being seduced by the collective.

Through acceptance of the God-image as a manifestation of our Collective Self's quest for wholeness, we and our gods have the potential to become truly moral. We have explored some of the many theories of religious violence and a variety of prescriptions for a cure. Solutions proposed range widely, including ideas like rejecting monotheism, purging sacred texts of violent passages, armed state intervention, revision of government policy in handling terrorists, globalization of American religious pluralism, and even advocating removing all taint of religion from politics. These prescriptions, like the explanations linked with them, do shed light on aspects of the problem, but they do not reach the heart of the matter. In terms of solutions, some of the suggestions are too global and impracticable for most of us to gain any sense of agency in the face of this devastating problem.

The impossibility of prescriptions that advocate evacuation of all religious thought from the political realm are especially problematic, although perhaps not obviously so for those of us shaped by Western democratic ideals. Regardless of one's political or religious affiliations, religion simply cannot be segregated from politics. For the truly religious individual, all of life is informed by faith. Religions are meaning-making systems and as such necessarily inform *all* aspects of life, politics included. As previously noted, Gandhi astutely observed that anyone who believes religion and politics have nothing to do with one another understands neither religion nor politics.

While in prison awaiting execution by the Nazis, German Protestant Christian theologian Dietrich Bonheoffer (1906–1945) wrote that "the world that has come of age is more godless, and perhaps for that very reason nearer to God, than the world before its coming of age. . . . Our coming of age leads us to a true recognition of our situation before God."[27] Echoing the thesis that the Western God-image is evolving, he wrote,

> The God who lets us live in the world without the hypothesis of God is the God before whom we stand continually. Before God and with God we live without God. God lets himself be pushed out of the world on to the cross. He is weak and powerless in the world, and that is precisely the way, the only way, in which he is with us and helps us.[28]

The historical and evolutionary forces that lead us to a "world come of age" liberate us also from a false image of God and open the way for a new understanding of the meaning and function of religion. Religion properly understood is not uncritical belief and unquestioning obedience to authoritative leaders.

Likewise, Jung believed that true religion is not creed, which is what those who advocate the separation of religion from politics actually seem to mean. "Creeds are codified and dogmatized forms of original religious experience . . . congealed in a rigid, often elaborate structure"—religious teachings reified, in other words.[29] It is something else entirely. Religion is "a kind of attitude which takes careful and conscientious account of certain numinous feelings, ideas, and events,"[30] a feeling of utter dependence and a taste for the

Infinite. Religious feeling takes hold of the human in such a way that we are "always rather [the numinosum's] victim than its creator."[31] And if the Self archetype is the God-within, we truly are *homo religiosus*; to deny this is to deny the inner reality of human existence.

The history of the United States illustrates the impossibility of evacuating religion from the political arena. In the U.S. political system, the concept of separation of church and state is central, and diverse religious ideologies co-exist in relative peace. As previously noted, Rodney Stark believes that religious civility in America is a product of pluralism: "The key to high levels of local religious commitment and of religious civility is not fewer religions, but more."[32] Archetypal psychology helps us understand why this seems to be so. In American culture a distinctive form of *civil religion* has evolved in which references to God are politically acceptable and important symbols of our culture (e.g., the Declaration of Independence and the flag) are imbued with a sacred character. Religion as practiced in America has become more civil (in the sense of being courteous toward other religions) precisely because there has evolved a manifestation of the collective American Self that allows believers of diverse *creeds* to adopt a common *religion*, as defined in Jungian terms. This does not mean that the only solution to the problem of religious violence is the American style of government and culture. Anytime a collective Self becomes elevated to the point of absolutist claims, the same disastrous dynamics are put into play. Sadly, American attitudes have recently begun to show signs of problematic ego inflation leading to violence fueled by claims that the only legitimate form of government is the American form. Political rhetoric in America has taken on tones reminiscent of evangelical religious fervor in the insistence among some currently in power that democracy and capitalism must be spread the world over. Human beings construct gods out of ideologies, be they religious or political; all false gods must be transformed if there is to be an end to killing those who disagree with us.

The transformation of our collective unconscious God-images may only happen through the work of individuals willing to take on the arduous task of individuation and courageous enough to challenge groups when Shadow projections threaten relations with outsiders. In a 1939 interview, on the verge of Germany's invasion of Poland, Jung said, "The world problem starts with the individual. . . . Attend to your private and personal conflicts and you will be reducing by one millionth millionth the world conflict."[33] Religious expression, including the God-image, is always born of the interplay between public and private realties. The unconscious "thinks" in images generated in response to the conscious situation. The task that faces each of us is to develop a wider consciousness though which we "divest the self of the false wrappings of the persona on the one hand, and of the suggestive power of primordial images [the archetypes] on the other."[34]

Humanity is on the whole not nearly as good as we want or imagine ourselves to be. Collectivities like religious groups carry within a spirit that is
shaped by the accumulated deep-seated emotional patterns and unacknowledged thoughts of individuals, and so the problems of groups are always the
result of accumulated individual evils.[35] Since the most powerful "psychological fact" in a system is the god, the inflation that results from identification of the ego with the Self or image of God-within leads to lust for power.
*This* is the source of aggression in the name of our gods, for "where love
stops, power begins, and violence, and terror."[36]

The lust for ascendancy that has marred humanity's religious expression is a
symptom of the "spiritual problem of modern [humanity]" that "shows itself in
our inner life by the shattering of our faith in ourselves and our own worth." We
have "lost all metaphysical certainties" and yet we long for them and so have
"set up in their place the ideals of material security." The old gods have failed
us, so we have created new ones. "The upheaval of our world and the upheaval
in consciousness is one and the same. . . . An enormous tension has arisen between the opposite poles of outer and inner life, between objective and subjective reality."[37] This strain is reflected in the perceived conflict between religion
and science, spiritual values and technological capabilities. In the scramble to
find new gods, some deny the darker side of human nature and of our images
of the Transcendent while actively projecting this unacknowledged darkness
onto others. The conflict can only be resolved for an individual or culture by
consciously acknowledging our individual and collective Shadow archetypes in
the process of working toward psychological wholeness. This truly is an accomplishment achieved only through "eternal vigilance."

Transcendent realities are not accessible to human experience, only their
psychic manifestations are. Archetypal psychology warns us that "psychical
dangers are much more dangerous than epidemics or earthquakes."[38] We cannot *know* the origin of our psychological images of the Transcendent. No one
of us, no group of us, knows the mind of God. Honest acknowledgement of
this is the first step toward genuine religious peace.

> The only thing that really matters now is whether [humanity] can climb up to a
> higher moral level, to a higher plane of consciousness, in order to be equal to the
> superhuman powers which the fallen angels have played into [our] hands.[39]

We must become more moral than our gods.

## NOTES

1. Carnegie Commission on Preventing Deadly Conflict, *Preventing Deadly Conflict: Final Report with Executive Summary* (Washington, DC: Author, 1997), 25.

2. Some of the ideas set forth here first appeared in print in Charlene Burns, "A Jungian Perspective on Religious Violence and Personal Responsibility," *Crosscurrents* 56 (Spring 2006): 16–24.

3. C. G. Jung, *The Archetypes and the Collective Unconscious*, in *The Collected Works*, trans. R. F. C. Hull, ed. H. Read, M. Fordham, G. Adler, and W. McGuire, vol. 9/1, Bollingen Series 20 (Princeton, NJ: Princeton University Press, 1968/1980), 349.

4. Jung, *Archetypes*, 349.

5. C. G. Jung, *Aion: Researches into the Phenomenology of the Self*, trans. R. F. C. Hull, ed. H. Read, M. Fordham, G Adler, and W. McGuire, vol. 9/2, Bollingen Series 20 (Princeton, NJ: Princeton University Press, 1959/1969), 109.

6. C. G. Jung, *Modern Man in Search of a Soul*, trans. W. S. Dell and C. F. Baynes (San Diego: Harcourt Brace Jovanovich, 1933), 142–43.

7. C. G. Jung, *C. G. Jung Speaking: Interviews and Encounters*, ed. William McGuire and R. F. C. Hull, Bollingen Series 97 (Princeton, NJ: Princeton University Press, 1977), 136–39.

8. Philip Zimbardo, "Pathology of Imprisonment," *Society* 9 (1972): 6; quoted in James Waller, *Becoming Evil: How Ordinary People Commit Genocide and Mass Killing*, 2nd ed. (New York: Oxford University Press, 2007), 231.

9. C. G. Jung, *Letters*, trans. R. F. C. Hull, ed. Gerhard Adler and Aniela Jaffé, vol. 2, Bollingen Series 95 (Princeton, NJ: Princeton University Press, 1973), 311; cited in Edward F. Edinger, *The New God-Image: A Study of Jung's Key Letters Concerning the Evolution of the Western God-Image*, ed. Diane D. Cordic and Charles Yates (Wilmette, IL: Chiron Publications, 1996), 71.

10. Seyyed Hossein Nasr, *The Garden of Truth: The Vision and Promise of Sufism, Islam's Mystical Tradition* (New York: Harper Collins, 2007), 135, 158.

11. Seyyed Hossein Nasr, *Sufi Essays* (Albany, NY: SUNY Press, 1972), 38–49.

12. Nasr, *Sufi Essays*, 71.

13. Seyyed Hossein Nasr, *Ideal and Realities of Islam* (New York: Praeger, 1967), 72, 77, 94, 97.

14. M. Fethullah Gülen, *Toward a Global Civilization of Love and Tolerance* (Somerset, NJ: The Light, 2006), 187.

15. Gregory Palamas, *Triads* III, 2 § 24, in John Meyendorff, *St. Gregory Palamas and Orthodox Spirituality*, trans. Adele Fiske. (Crestwood, NY: St. Vladimir Press, 1998).

16. Meister Eckhart, *The Essential Sermons, Commentaries, Treatises and Defense*, trans. and ed. Bernard McGinn and Edmund Colledge (New York: Paulist Press, 1981).

17. J. Brent Bill, *Holy Silence: The Gift of Quaker Spirituality* (Brewster, MA: Paraclete Press, 2006), 7–8.

18. Moshe Idel, "Universalization and Integration: Two Conceptions of Mystical Union in Judaism," in *Mystical Union in Judaism, Christianity, and Islam: An Ecumenical Dialogue*, ed. Moshe Idel and Bernard McGinn (New York: Continuum Press, 1996), 50–52.

19. Gershom Scholem, *On the Mystical Shape of the Godhead* (New York: Schocken Books, 1991), 243.

20. David Ariel, *Kabbalah: The Mystical Quest in Judaism* (Lanham, MD: Rowman & Littlefield, 2006).

21. Darrel J. Fasching and Dell Dechant, *Comparative Religious Ethics: A Narrative Approach* (Oxford, UK: Blackwell Press, 2001), 56–70, 75–83.

22. Gerhard Ebling, *Luther: An Introduction to His Thought* (Philadelphia: Fortress Press, 1970), 236.

23. Eckhart Society, "Eckhart von Hockheim," www.eckhartsociety.org/meister.htm (accessed January 6, 2008).

24. James Hillman, *A Terrible Love of War* (New York: Penguin Books, 2004), 191.

25. Walter Wink, *Unmasking the Powers: The Invisible Forces that Determine Human Existence* (Minneapolis: Fortress Press, 1986), 4–5.

26. Religion as either life affirming or demonic is from Lloyd Steffen, *Holy War, Just War: Exploring the Moral Meaning of Religious Violence* (Lanham, MD: Rowman & Littlefield, 2007).

27. Dietrich Bonhoeffer, *Letters and Papers from Prison*, trans. Reginald Fuller, ed. Eberhard Bethge (New York: Macmillan, 1972), 362, 360.

28. Bonhoeffer, *Letters and Papers*, 129.

29. C. G. Jung, *Psychology and Religion: The Terry Lectures* (New Haven, CT: Yale University Press, 1938/1966), 6.

30. C. G. Jung, letter to Pastor Tanner; quoted in Edinger, *New God-Image*, 142.

31. Jung, *Psychology and Religion*, 4.

32. Rodney Stark, *One True God: Historical Consequences of Monotheism* (Princeton, NJ: Princeton University Press, 2001), 259.

33. Jung, *C. G. Jung Speaking*, 140.

34. C. G. Jung, "Relations between the Ego and the Unconscious," in *The Portable Jung*, ed. Joseph Campbell (New York: Penguin Press, 1928/1976), 123.

35. "In as much as collectivities are mere accumulations of individuals, their problems are also accumulations of individual problems." Jung, *Psychology and Religion*, 95.

36. C. G. Jung, *The Undiscovered Self*, trans. R. F. C. Hull (New York: New American Library, 1958), 118.

37. Jung, *Modern Man*, 196, 204, 208, 211, 220.

38. Jung, *Psychology and Religion*, 11.

39. C. G. Jung, *Answer to Job*, in *The Portable Jung*, ed. Joseph Campbell (New York: Penguin Press, 1952/1976), 638.

# Bibliography

Adolphson, Mikael S. *The Teeth and Claws of the Buddha: Monastic Warriors and Sōhei in Japanese History*. Honolulu: University of Hawaii Press, 2007.

Aho, James A. *Religious Mythology and the Art of War: Comparative Religious Symbolisms of Military Violence*. Westport, CT: Greenwood Press, 1981.

Ariel, David. *Kabbalah: The Mystical Quest in Judaism*. Lanham, MD: Rowman & Littlefield, 2006.

Astour, Michael. "841 B.C.: The First Assyrian Invasion of Israel." *Journal of the American Oriental Society* 91, no. 3 (July–September 1971): 383–89.

Atran, Scott. *In Gods We Trust: The Evolutionary Landscape of Religion*. New York: Oxford University Press, 2002.

Avalos, Hector. *Fighting Words: The Origins of Religious Violence*. New York: Prometheus, 2005.

———. "Rethinking Religious Violence." In *The Just War and Jihad: Violence in Judaism, Christianity, and Islam*, edited by R. Joseph Hoffmann, 99–109. Amherst, NY: Prometheus, 2006.

Bainton, Roland H. *Christian Attitudes toward War and Peace*. Nashville: Abingdon Press, 1960.

Baumeister, Roy F. *Evil: Inside Human Violence and Cruelty*. New York: Owl Books, 1999.

Berger, Peter L. "The Desecularization of the World: A Global Overview." In *The Desecularization of the World: Resurgent Religion and World Politics*, edited by Peter L. Berger, 1–18. Washington, DC: Ethics and Public Policy Center and Wm. B. Eerdmans, 1999.

———. *The Sacred Canopy: Elements of a Sociological Theory of Religion*. Garden City, NY: Doubleday, 1967.

Berger, Peter L., and Thomas Luckmann. *The Social Construction of Reality: A Treatise in the Sociology of Knowledge*. New York: Anchor Books, 1967.

Berger, Peter L., and Stanley Pullberg. "Reification and the Sociological Critique of Consciousness." *History and Theory* 4, no. 2 (1965): 196–211.

133

*Bhagavad Gita*. Translated by Barbara Stoler Miller. New York: Bantam Books, 1986.

Bill, J. Brent. *Holy Silence: The Gift of Quaker Spirituality*. Brewster, MA: Paraclete Press, 2006.

Bishop, Paul. "C.G. Jung and 'Naturmystik': The Early Poem 'Gedanken In Einer Frühlingsnacht.'" *German Life and Letters* 56, no. 4 (October 2003): 327–43.

———. *Jung's Answer to Job: A Commentary*. New York: Brunner-Routledge, 2002.

Blass, Thomas. *The Man Who Shocked the World*. New York: Basic Books, 2004.

Bonhoeffer, Dietrich. *Letters and Papers from Prison*. Translated by Reginald Fuller. Edited by Eberhard Bethge. New York: Macmillan, 1972.

Boyer, Pascal. *Religion Explained: The Evolutionary Origins of Religious Thought*. New York: Basic Books, 2001.

Bruner, Jerome. *Acts of Meaning*. Cambridge, MA: Harvard University Press, 1990.

Burns, Charlene. "A Jungian Perspective on Religious Violence and Personal Responsibility." *CrossCurrents* 56 (Spring 2006): 16–24.

Bushman, Brad J., and Roy F. Baumeister. "Threatened Egotism, Narcissism, Self-Esteem, and Direct and Displaced Aggression: Does Self-Love or Self-Hate Lead to Violence?" *Journal of Personality and Social Psychology* 75, no. 1 (1998): 219–29.

Carnegie Commission on Preventing Deadly Conflict. *Preventing Deadly Conflict: Final Report with Executive Summary*. Washington, DC: Author, 1997.

Center for Strategic and International Studies (CSIS). "What Is Globalization?" www.globalization101.org/What_is_Globalization.html (accessed March 3, 2007).

Childress, James F. "Moral Discourse about War in the Early Church." *Journal of Religious Ethics* 12, no. 1 (January 2006): 2–18.

Cohen, E. D. *C. G. Jung and the Scientific Attitude*. New York: Philosophical Library, 1975.

Cook, David. *Understanding Jihad*. Berkeley: University of California Press, 2005.

Corbett, Lionel. "Kohut and Jung: A Comparison of Theory and Therapy." In *Self Psychology: Comparisons and Contrasts*, edited by Douglas W. Detrick and Susan B. Detrick. Hillsdale, NJ: Analytic Press, 1989. www.findingstone.com/professionals/monographs/kohutandjung.htm (accessed August 7, 2007).

Crouter, Richard. "Introduction." In *On Religion: Speeches to Its Cultured Despisers*, by Friedrich Schleiermacher. Translated by Richard Crouter. Cambridge: Cambridge University Press, 1988.

Dawkins, Richard. *The Devil's Chaplain*. London: Weidenfield & Nicolson, 2003.

———. *The God Delusion*. New York: Bantam Books, 2006.

Donald, Merlin. *A Mind So Rare: The Evolution of Human Consciousness*. New York: W. W. Norton, 2001.

Dourley, John P. "The Religious Significance of Jung's Psychology." *International Journal for the Psychology of Religion* 5, no. 2 (1995): 73–89.

Dundas, Paul. *The Jains*. London: Routledge, 1992.

Ebling, Gerhard. *Luther: An Introduction to His Thought*. Philadelphia: Fortress Press, 1970.

Eckhart, Meister. *The Essential Sermons, Commentaries, Treatises and Defense*. Translated and edited by Bernard McGinn and Edmund Colledge. New York: Paulist Press, 1981.

Eckhart Society. "Eckhart von Hockheim," www.eckhartsociety.org/meister.htm (accessed January 6, 2008).

Edinger, Edward F. *Ego and Archetype: Individuation and the Religious Function of the Psyche*. Boston: Shambala, 1992.

———. *The New God-Image: A Study of Jung's Key Letters Concerning the Evolution of the Western God-Image*. Edited by Diane D. Cordic and Charles Yates. Wilmette, IL: Chiron Publications, 1996.

Erickson, Eric H. *Childhood and Society*. New York: W. W. Norton, 1950.

Evans, Michael. *Beyond Iraq: The Next Move—Ancient Prophecy and Modern-Day Conspiracy Collide*. Lakeland, FL: White Stone Books, 2003.

Fasching, Darrel J., and Dell Dechant. *Comparative Religious Ethics: A Narrative Approach*. Oxford, UK: Blackwell Press, 2001.

Ferguson, John. *War and Peace in the World's Religions*. New York: Oxford University Press, 1978.

Fordham, Michael. *New Developments in Analytical Psychology*. London: Routledge & Kegan Paul, 1957.

Förster, Eckhart. "Is There a 'Gap' in Kant's Critical System?" *Journal of the History of Philosophy* 25, no. 4 (October 1987): 533–55.

Fox, Jonathan. *Religion, Civilization, and Civil War: 1945 through the New Millennium*. Lanham, MD: Lexington Books, 2004.

———. "The Rise of Religious Nationalism and Conflict: Ethnic Conflict and Revolutionary Wars 1945–2001." *Journal of Peace Research* 41 (2004): 715–33.

Freud, Sigmund. *Civilization and Its Discontents*. New York: W. W. Norton, 1930/1989.

———. *The Future of an Illusion*. New York: W. W. Norton, 1927/1989.

Friedman, Richard Elliott. *The Disappearance of God: A Divine Mystery*. Boston: Little, Brown, 1995.

Gabel, Peter. "Reification in Legal Reasoning." In *Research in Law and Sociology*, edited by S. Spencer. Vol. 3. Greenwich, CT: JAI Press, 1980.

Gandhi, Mohandas K. *The Teaching of the Gita*. Bombay: Bharatiya Vidya Bhavan, 1971.

Gernet, Jacques. *Buddhism in Chinese Society: An Economic History from the Fifth to the Tenth Century*. Translated by F. Verellen. New York: Columbia University Press, 1998.

Gillett, Eric. "The Confusion over Personification and Reification." *Psychoanalysis and Contemporary Thought* 16, no. 1 (1993): 3–42.

Gombrich, Richard. "Is the Sri Lankan War a Buddhist Fundamentalism?" In *Buddhism, Conflict and Violence in Modern Sri Lanka*, edited by Mahinda Deegalle. London: Routledge, 2006.

Gorenberg, Gershon. *The End of Days: Fundamentalism and the Struggle for the Temple Mount*. New York: Free Press, 2000.

Gotchev, Atanas. "Terrorism and Globalization." In *The Roots of Terrorism*, edited by Louise Richardson, 103–15. New York: Routledge, 2006.

Greenberg, Jeff, Linda Simon, Tom Pyszczynski, Sheldon Solomon, and Dan Chatel. "Terror Management and Tolerance: Does Mortality Salience Always Intensify

Negative Reactions to Others Who Threaten One's Worldview?" *Journal of Personality and Social Psychology* 63 (1992): 212–20.

Gülen, M. Fethullah. *Toward a Global Civilization of Love and Tolerance*. Somerset, NJ: The Light, 2006.

Gurr, Ted Robert. "Economic Factors." In *The Roots of Terrorism*, edited by Louise Richardson, 85–100. New York: Routledge, 2006.

Hanh, Thich Nhat. *Transformation and Healing: Sutra on the Four Establishments of Mindfulness*. Berkeley, CA: Parallax Press, 1990.

Harris, Rabia Terri. "Nonviolence in Islam: The Alternative Community Tradition." In *Subverting Hatred: The Challenge of Nonviolence in Religious Traditions*, edited by Daniel L. Smith-Christopher, 95–113. Maryknoll, NY: Orbis Books, 1998.

Hillman, James. *A Terrible Love of War*. New York: Penguin Books, 2004.

Homans, Peter. *Jung in Context: Modernity and the Making of Psychology*. Chicago: University of Chicago Press, 1979/1995.

Housley, Norman. *Contesting the Crusades*. Malden, MA: Blackwell Publishing, 2006.

Hudson, Rex A. *Who Becomes a Terrorist and Why: The 1999 Government Report on Profiling Terrorists*. Guilford, CT: Lyons Press, 1999.

Idel, Moshe. "Universalization and Integration: Two Conceptions of Mystical Union in Judaism." In *Mystical Union in Judaism, Christianity, and Islam: An Ecumenical Dialogue*, edited by Moshe Idel and Bernard McGinn, 27–58. New York: Continuum Press, 1996.

Jones, James W. *Terror and Transformation: The Ambiguity of Religion in Psychoanalytic Perspective*. New York: Routledge, 2002.

———. "Why Does Religion Turn Violent? A Psychoanalytic Exploration of Religious Terrorism." *Psychoanalytic Review* 93, no. 2 (April 2006): 167–90.

Josephus. *The New Complete Works of Josephus*. Translated by William Whiston. Grand Rapids, MI: Kregel Academic & Professional, 1999.

Jubair, Salah. *Bangsamoro—A Nation Under Endless Tyranny*. Lahore, Pakistan: Islamic Research Academy, 1984.

Jung, C. G. *Aion: Researches into the Phenomenology of the Self*. Translated by R. F. C. Hull. Edited by H. Read, M. Fordham, G Adler, and W. McGuire. Vol. 9/2. Bollingen Series 20. Princeton, NJ: Princeton University Press, 1959/1969.

———. *Answer to Job*. In *The Portable Jung*, edited by Joseph Campbell, 519–650. New York: Penguin Press, 1952/1976.

———. *The Archetypes and the Collective Unconscious*. In *The Collected Works*. Translated by R. F. C. Hull. Edited by H. Read, M. Fordham, G. Adler, and W. McGuire. Vol. 9/1. Bollingen Series 20. Princeton, NJ: Princeton University Press, 1968/1980.

———. *C. G. Jung Speaking: Interviews and Encounters*. Edited by William McGuire and R. F. C. Hull. Bollingen Series 97. Princeton, NJ: Princeton University Press, 1977.

———. *The Collected Works*. Translated by R. F. C. Hull. Edited by H. Read, M. Fordham, G. Adler, and W. McGuire. 20 vols. Bollingen Series. Princeton, NJ: Princeton University Press, 1953–1983.

———. *Letters*. Translated by R. F. C. Hull. Edited by Gerhard Adler and Aniela Jaffé. Bollingen Series 95:1–2. Princeton, NJ: Princeton University Press, 1973.

———. *Letters, 1906–1950*. Translated by R. F. C. Hull. Edited by Gerhard Adler and Aniela Jaffé. London: Routledge & Kegan Paul, 1973.

———. *Letters, 1951–1961*. Translated by R. F. C. Hull. Edited by Gerhard Adler and Aniela Jaffé. London: Routledge & Kegan Paul, 1975.

———. *Memories, Dreams, Reflections*. Translated by Richard and Clara Winston. Edited by Aniela Jaffé. New York: Vintage Books, 1961/1989.

———. "Mind and Earth." In *The Collected Works*. Translated by R. F. C. Hull. Edited by H. Read, M. Fordham, G. Adler, and W. McGuire. Vol. 10. Bollingen Series. Princeton, NJ: Princeton University Press, 1927/1931.

———. *Modern Man in Search of a Soul*. Translated by W. S. Dell and C. F. Baynes. San Diego: Harcourt Brace Jovanovich, 1933.

———. "On the Nature of the Psyche." In *The Collected Works*. Translated by R. F. C. Hull. Edited by H. Read, M. Fordham, G. Adler, and W. McGuire. Vol. 8. Bollingen Series. Princeton, NJ: Princeton University Press, 1947/1954.

———. *Psychology and Alchemy*. In *The Collected Works*. Translated by R. F. C. Hull. Edited by H. Read, M. Fordham, G. Adler, and W. McGuire. Vol. 12. Bollingen Series. Princeton, NJ: Princeton University Press, 1980.

———. *Psychology and Religion: The Terry Lectures*. New Haven, CT: Yale University Press, 1938/1966.

———. "Relations between the Ego and the Unconscious." In *The Portable Jung*, edited by Joseph Campbell, 70–138. New York: Penguin Press, 1928/1976.

———. "The Shadow." In *The Collected Works*. Translated by R. F. C. Hull. Edited by H. Read, M. Fordham, G. Adler, and W. McGuire. Vol. 9/2. Bollingen Series. Princeton, NJ: Princeton University Press, 1953–1983.

———. *The Structure and Dynamics of the Psyche*. In *The Collected Works*. Translated by R. F. C. Hull. Edited by H. Read, M. Fordham, G. Adler, and W. McGuire, paras. 283–342. Vol. 8. Bollingen Series. Princeton, NJ: Princeton University Press, 1953–1983.

———. *Two Essays in Analytical Psychology*. In *The Collected Works*. Translated by R. F. C. Hull. Edited by H. Read, M. Fordham, G. Adler, and W. McGuire. Vol. 7. Bollingen Series 20. Princeton, NJ: Princeton University Press, 1966.

———. *The Undiscovered Self*. Translated by R. F. C. Hull. New York: New American Library, 1958.

Jurgensmeyer, Mark. "Religion as a Cause for Terrorism." In *The Roots of Terrorism*, edited by Louise Richardson, 133–44. New York: Routledge, 2006.

———. *Terror in the Mind of God: The Global Rise of Religious Violence*. Berkeley: University of California Press, 2000.

Keim, Paul. "Is God Non-Violent?" *Conrad Grabel Review* 21, no. 1 (Winter 2003): 25–32.

Kilborne, Benjamin. "Fields of Shame: Anthropologists Abroad." *Ethos* 20, no. 2 (June 1992): 230–53.

Kimball, Charles. *When Religion Becomes Evil: Five Warning Signs*. San Francisco: Harper San Francisco, 2002.

Kohut, Heinz. *The Analysis of the Self*. New York: International Universities Press, 1971.

——. *How Does Analysis Cure?* Chicago: Chicago University Press, 1984.

——. "Forms and Transformations of Narcissism." *Journal of the American Psychoanalytic Association* 14 (1966): 243–72.

——. "Narcissism and Narcissistic Rage." In *The Psychoanalytic Study of the Child*, 377–86. New York: Quadrangle Press, 1972.

——. *The Restoration of the Self.* New York: International Universities Press, 1977.

Kraft, Kenneth, ed. *Inner Peace, World Peace: Essays on Buddhism and Nonviolence*. New York: SUNY Press, 1992.

Lefebvre, Henri. *The Production of Space*. Translated by Donald Nicholson Smith. Cambridge, MA: Blackwell, 1991.

Lewis, Bernard. *The Assassins: A Radical Sect in Islam*. New York: Basic Books, 1968/2002.

Lifton, Robert Jay. *The Future of Immortality*. New York: Basic Books, 1987.

——. *The Nazi Doctors: Medicalized Killing and the Psychology of Genocide*. New York: Basic Books, 1986.

Ling, Trevor. *Buddhism, Imperialism, and War*. London: George Allen & Unwin, 1979.

Lobe, Jim. "Conservative Christians Biggest Backers of Iraq War." CommonDreams.org, October 12, 2002, www.commondreams.org/headlines02/1010-02.htm (accessed January 3, 2008).

Luther, Martin. *Luther's Works*. Edited by Jaroslav Pelikan. Saint Louis, MO: Concordia, 1955.

MacIntyre, Ferren. "Was Religion a Kinship Surrogate?" *Journal of the American Academy of Religion* 72, no. 3 (2004): 653–94.

May, Christopher. "The Denial of History: Reification, Intellectual Property Rights, and the Lessons of the Past." *Class and Capital* 88 (March 2006): 33–56.

McAlister, Elizabeth. "Globalization and the Religious Production of Space." *Journal for the Scientific Study of Religion* 44, no. 3 (2005): 249–55.

McCauley, Clark. "Psychological Issues in Understanding Terrorism and the Response to Terrorism." In *Psychology of Terrorism: Condensed Edition*, edited by Chris E. Stout, 34–65. Westport, CT: Praeger, 2004.

McDermott, Terry. *Perfect Soldiers: The Hijackers: Who They Were, Why They Did It*. New York: Harper Collins, 2005.

McTernan, Oliver. *Violence in God's Name: Religion in an Age of Conflict*. Maryknoll, NY: Orbis Press, 2003.

Miles, Jack. *God: A Biography*. New York: Knopf, 1995.

Milgram, Stanley. *Obedience to Authority: An Experimental View*. New York: Harper & Row, 1974.

Milgrom, Jeremy. "'Let Your Love for Me Vanquish Your Hatred for Him': Nonviolence and Modern Judaism." In *Subverting Hatred: The Challenge of Nonviolence in Religious Traditions*, edited by Daniel L. Smith-Christopher, 115–39. Maryknoll, NY: Orbis Books, 1998.

Moghaddam, Fathali M. *From the Terrorists' Point of View: What They Experience and Why They Come to Destroy*. Westport, CT: Praeger Security International, 2006.

Monroe, Robert L. *Facing the Dragon: Confronting Personal and Spiritual Grandiosity*. Wilmette, IL: Chiron Publications, 2003.

Muraven, Mark, and Roy F. Baumeister. "Suicide, Sex, Terror, Paralysis, and Other Pitfalls of Reductionist Self-Preservation Theory." *Psychological Inquiry* 8, no. 1 (1997): 36–40.

Nagy, Marilyn. *Philosophical Issues in the Psychology of C. G. Jung*. Albany, NY: SUNY Press, 1991.

Nasr, Seyyed Hossein. *The Garden of Truth: The Vision and Promise of Sufism, Islam's Mystical Tradition*. New York: Harper Collins, 2007.

——. *Sufi Essays*. Albany, NY: SUNY Press, 1972.

——. *Ideal and Realities of Islam*. New York: Praeger, 1967.

Nelson-Pallmeyer, Jack. *Is Religion Killing Us? Violence in the Bible and the Quran*. New York: Trinity Press International, 2003.

Noll, Richard. *The Jung Cult: Origins of a Charismatic Movement*. Princeton, NJ: Princeton University Press, 1994.

Obeyesekere, Gananath. "Buddhism, Ethnicity, and Identity: A Problem in Buddhist History." In *Buddhism: Conflict and Violence in Modern Sri Lanka*, edited by Mahinda Deegalle, 134–62. London: Routledge, 2006.

Oommen, T. K. "Religion as Source of Violence: A Sociological Perspective." *Ecumenical Review* 53, no. 2 (2001): 168–78.

Opeloye, Muhib O. "Injustice in the World Order: The Revolution of Islamic Republic of Iran as a Response." In *Imam Kohmeini and the International System: A Collection of Articles*, translated by Mansoor Limba, 146–58. Tehran, Iran: Institute for Compilation and Publication of Imam Khomeini's Works, 2004. www.geocities.com/icpikw/intlsystem11_08.pdf (accessed March 30, 2007).

Ornes, Stephen. "Radioactive Boy Scout: Teenager Achieves Nuclear Fusion at Home." *Discover Magazine*, http://discovermagazine.com/2007/mar/radioactive-boy-scout.3.06.2007 (accessed March 30, 2007).

O'Shea, Stephen. *The Perfect Heresy: The Revolutionary Life and Death of the Medieval Cathars*. New York: Walker & Co, 2001.

Palamas, Gregory. *Triads* III, 2 § 24. In John Meyendorff, *St. Gregory Palamas and Orthodox Spirituality*, translated by Adele Fiske. Crestwood, NY: St. Vladimir Press, 1998.

Palmer, Michael. *Freud and Jung on Religion*. London: Routledge, 1997.

Papadopoulos, Renos K. "Jung's Epistemology and Methodology." In *The Handbook of Jungian Psychology: Theory, Practice, and Applications*, edited by Renos K. Papadopoulos, 7–53. London: Routledge, 2006.

Pape, Robert. "Conversations with History." Institute of International Studies, UC Berkeley. http://globetrotter.berkeley.edu/people6/Pape/pape-con0.html (accessed March 2, 2007).

——. *Dying to Win: The Strategic Logic of Suicide Terrorism*. New York: Random House, 2005.

Park, Crystal. "Religion and Meaning." In *Handbook of the Psychology of Religion and Spirituality*, edited by Raymond F. Paloutzian and Crystal Park, 295–314. New York: Guilford Press, 2005.

Patton, John. *Is Human Forgiveness Possible?* Nashville: Abingdon Press, 1985.
Pauloutzian, Ray. "Purpose in Life and Values Changes Following Conversion." *Journal of Personality and Social Psychology* 41 (1981): 1153–60.
Pratt, James B. "Religion and the Younger Generation." *Yale Review* 12 (1923): 594–613.
Puniyani, Ram. "Introduction." In *Religion, Power, and Violence: Expression of Politics in Contemporary Times*, edited by Ram Puniyani, 12–26. New Delhi, India: Sage, 2005.
——. "Religion: Opium of the Masses or . . . ." In *Religion, Power, and Violence: Expression of Politics in Contemporary Times*, edited by Ram Puniyani, 27–43. New Delhi, India: Sage, 2005.
Pyszczynski, Tom, Sheldon Solomon, and Jeff Greenberg. *In the Wake of 9/11: The Psychology of Terror*. Washington, DC: American Psychological Association, 2003.
Ralston, Holmes, III. "Review of Darwin's Cathedral: Evolution, Religion, and the Nature of Society." *Journal of the American Academy of Religion* 72, no. 3 (2004): 800–803.
Richardson, Louise. "The Roots of Terrorism: An Overview." In *The Roots of Terrorism*, edited by Louise Richardson, 1–16. Club de Madrid Series on Democracy and Terrorism, vol. 1. New York: Routledge, 2006.
Rose, Gilbert J. "The Creativity of Everyday Life." In *Between Fantasy and Reality: Transitional Objects and Phenomena*, edited by Simon Grolnick and Leonard Barkin, 347–62. New York: Jason Aronson, 1978.
Roy, Oliver. "Terrorism and Deculturation." In *The Roots of Terrorism*, edited by Louise Richardson, 159–70. New York: Routledge, 2006.
Sabbah, Patriarch Michel, Swerios Malki Mourad, Riah Abu El-Assal, and Munib Younan. "The Jerusalem Declaration on Christian Zionism." August 22, 2006. www.voltairenet.org/article144310.html (accessed April 4, 2007).
Sachedina, Abdulaziz Abdulhussein. *Islamic Messianism: The Idea of the Mahdi in Twelver Shi`ism*. Albany, NY: SUNY Press, 1981.
Saritoprak, Zeki. "An Islamic Approach to Peace and Nonviolence: A Turkish Experience." *Muslim World* 95 (July 2005): 413–27.
Schleiermacher, Friedrich. *The Christian Faith*. Edited by H. R. MacIntosh and J. S. Stewart. Edinburgh: T & T Clark, 1989.
——. *Dialectic, or the Art of Doing Philosophy: A Study of the 1811 Notes*. Translated by Terrence N. Tice. Atlanta: Scholar's Press, 1996.
——. *On Religion: Speeches to its Cultured Despisers*. Translated by John Oman. Louisville, KY: Westminster John Knox Press, 1994.
Scholem, Gershom. *Kabbalah*. New York: Dorset Press, 1987.
——. *On the Mystical Shape of the Godhead*. New York: Schocken Books, 1991.
Schwartz, Regina M. *The Curse of Cain: The Violent Legacy of Monotheism*. Chicago: University of Chicago Press, 1997.
Scruton, Roger. *Kant: A Very Short Introduction*. Oxford: Oxford University Press, 2001.
Selengut, Charles. *Sacred Fury: Understanding Religious Violence*. Walnut Creek, CA: AltaMira Press, 2003.

Sharma, Jyotirmaya. *Hindutva: Exploring the Idea of Hindu Nationalism*. New Delhi, India: Penguin Books India, 2003.

Silberman, Israela. "Religious Violence, Terrorism, and Peace." In *Handbook of the Psychology of Religion and Spirituality*, edited by Raymond Paloutzian and Crystal Park, 529–49. New York: Guilford, 2005.

Smith, Brian K. "Hinduism." In *God's Rule: The Politics of World Religions*, edited by Jacob Neusner, 185–212. Washington, DC: Georgetown University Press, 2003.

Solomon, Sheldon, Jeff Greenberg, and Tom Pyszczynski. "Return of the Living Dead." *Psychological Inquiry* 8, no. 3 (1977): 59–71.

Stark, Rodney. *One True God: Historical Consequences of Monotheism*. Princeton, NJ: Princeton University Press, 2001.

Steffen, Lloyd. *Holy War, Just War: Exploring the Moral Meaning of Religious Violence*. Lanham, MD: Rowman & Littlefield, 2007.

Stevens, Anthony. "The Archetypes." In *The Handbook of Jungian Psychology: Theory, Practice, and Applications*, edited by Renos K. Papadopoulos, 74–93. London: Routledge, 2006.

Strenger, Carlo. *Between Hermeneutics and Science: An Essay on the Epistemology of Psychoanalysis*. Madison, CT: International Universities Press, 1991.

Tambiah, Stanley J. *Buddhism Betrayed: Religion, Politics, and Violence in Sri Lanka*. Chicago: University of Chicago Press, 1992.

——. *Leveling Crowds: Ethnonationalist Conflicts and Collective Violence in South Asia*. Berkeley: University of California Press, 1997.

——. "Urban Riots and Cricket in South Asia: A Postscript to 'Leveling Crowds.'" *Modern Asian Studies* 39, no. 4 (2005): 897–927.

Thandeka. *The Embodied Self: Friedrich Schleiermacher's Solution to Kant's Problem of the Empirical Self*. Albany, NY: SUNY Press, 1995.

——. "Schleiermacher's 'Dialektik': The Discovery of the Self That Kant Lost." *Harvard Theological Review* 85, no. 4 (October 1992): 433–52.

Tillich, Paul. *Systematic Theology*, vol. 1. Chicago: University of Chicago Press, 1951.

Tomasello, Michael. *The Cultural Origins of Human Cognition*. Cambridge, MA: Harvard University Press, 1999.

Trible, Phyllis. *Texts of Terror: Literary-Feminist Readings of Biblical Narrative*. Philadelphia: Fortress Press, 1984.

Victoria, Brian Daizen. *Zen at War*. Lanham, MD: Rowman & Littlefield, 1997/2006.

Volf, Miroslav. "Divine Violence?" Letter to the editor. *Christian Century*, October 13, 1999.

Walker, Ken. "After the Coup: Missionaries Return to Begin Rebuilding out of the Rubble." *Christianity Today* 48, no. 5 (2004): 19.

Waller, James. *Becoming Evil: How Ordinary People Commit Genocide and Mass Killing*. 2nd ed. New York: Oxford University Press, 2007.

Whitehead, Alfred North. *Science and the Modern World*. New York: Macmillan, 1925.

Wilson, David Sloan. *Darwin's Cathedral: Evolution, Religion, and the Nature of Society*. Chicago: University of Chicago Press, 2002.

Wink, Walter. *Jesus and Nonviolence: A Third Way*. Minneapolis: Augsburg Fortress, 2003.

——. *Unmasking the Powers: The Invisible Forces that Determine Human Existence*. Minneapolis: Fortress Press, 1986.

Wood, Allen. *Kant. Blackwell "Great Minds" Series*. Edited by Steven Nadler. Malden, MA: Blackwell, 2005.

Wulff, David. "How Attached Should We Be to Attachment Theory?" *International Journal for the Psychology of Religion* 16 (January 2006): 29–36.

——. *Psychology of Religion: Classic and Contemporary*. 2nd ed. New York: John Wiley & Sons, 1997.

Yardley, Jonathan. "The 9/11 Hijackers." *Washington Post*, May 1, 2005, BW02.

Yoder, John Howard. "The Constantinian Sources of Western Social Ethics." In *The Priestly Kingdom: Social Ethics as Gospel*, 125–47. Notre Dame, IN: University of Notre Dame Press, 1984.

Younger, K. Lawson, Jr. "The Deportations of the Israelites." *Journal of Biblical Literature* 117, no. 2 (Summer 1998): 201–28.

Zimbardo, Philip. *The Lucifer Effect: Understanding How Good People Turn Evil*. New York: Random House, 2007.

——. "Pathology of Imprisonment." *Society* 9 (1972): 6.

# Index

emasculation, 38, 66–67, 81
enlightenment, 20–21, 72, 122–23
epistemology, xi, 80, 100–102, 107–109
ethnic cleansing, 61
ethnocentrism, vii, 65
evolution, biological, x, 16–17, 34–36, 59, 86

Fa-ch'ing, 20
Fox, Jonathan, 40–41
Freud, Sigmund, 33, 67, 80–82, 91–92
Friedman, Richard Elliott, 112–13
fundamentalism, 42

Gabel, Peter, 6
Gandhi, Mahatma, 4, 15, 39, 124, 128
Gefühl, xi, 104–108, 122
genocide, 57–64, 121
globalization, vii, ix–x, 7, 11, 36–38, 42–43, 65–67, 122, 128
God-image, xii, 34, 67, 94–95, 99, 108; transformation of, 109–14, 120–23, 127–30
group selection, biological, 34–35, 49
guilt, 81–85
Gülen, M. Fethullah, 28–29

Hanh, Thich Nhat, 22, 72
Haiti, and religious conflict, 47–48
heyschastic prayer, 124–25
Hinduism: nonviolence, 16, 124; violence, 13–16, 21–22, 29, 42, 47
Hindutva, 15–16, 42
Hitler, Adolph, 121
Holy War, 20–21, 24–27, 47
Homans, Peter, 92
humiliation, 38, 65–67, 81, 85, 94, 120–21. *See also* shame
idealization, xii, 67, 83–86, 120, 122
incarnation, xii, 106, 108–10, 114, 123
identity formation, 37, 65ff
individuation, 110, 112, 114, 122, 124, 126, 129–30
Iran, 37
Iraq, 126

Islam: nonviolence, 123–24; violence, viii, 13, 26–29, 37–38, 42, 44, 46–50, 65–66, 70
Israel, 16–19, 25–26, 28, 38, 40, 45–46, 113

Jainism, 29
Jerusalem, 17, 18, 45
Jihad, 26–27, 49–50, 65
Job, book of, 109–114
Jones, James W., xi, 85–86
Josephus, 17–18
Judaism, 113; nonviolence, 17–19, 125; violence, 4, 8–10, 16–19, 69–70
Jung, G. G., ix, xi–xii, 7, 79, 81, 86–95, 99–100, 119–132; as "demi-god," 115n1; epistemology, 100–14; historical context, 91–93
Jurgensmeyer, Mark, 38–41, 66–67, 81

Kant, Immanuel, xi, 100–107
"killing in order to heal," 126
King, Martin Luther, Jr., 7
Knights Templar, 24–25
Kohut, Heinz, 126
Khomeini, Ayatollah, 37–38

Luria, Isaac 125
Luther, Martin, 25, 70–71, 126
McCauley, Clark, 67
Mahdi, 27
Miles, Jack, 112
Milgram, Stanley, 62–64, 121–22
Mindanao, 48–49. *See also* Moro people
modernization, 33–34, 36–41, 66, 92, 121
monotheism, x, 9, 43–45, 47, 49, 128
moral geography, 47–48
moral disengagement, 57, 60–61, 74
Moro people, 48–50
mortality salience, 67–75
Muhammad, viii, 26–27, 44–45, 12
mysticism, 107

narcissism, ix, 73, 82–87, 89, 94, 126
Nasr, Seyyed Hossein, 123–24
nationalism, vii, 38, 41, 92, 120

# About the Author

Charlene P. E. Burns is associate professor of religious studies at the University of Wisconsin–Eau Claire. She has a Ph.D. in religion with a minor area concentration in the psychology of religion, and also has a degree in nursing. She is the author of *Divine Becoming: Rethinking Jesus and Incarnation*.